Everything We Thought Was Beautiful

Interviews with Radical Palestinian Women

Edited by Shoal Collective

SECOND EDITION

Everything We Thought Was Beautiful: Interviews with Radical Palestinian Women
Second edition

ISBN: 979-8-88744-145-0 (paperback)
ISBN: 979-8-88744-142-9 (hardcover)
ISBN: 979-8-88744-146-7 (ebook)
Library of Congress Control Number: 2025931261

Cover art by Zola
Cover design by John Yates / stealworks.com
Interior design by briandesign

10 9 8 7 6 5 4 3 2 1

PM Press
PO Box 23912
Oakland, CA 94623
www.pmpress.org

Printed in the USA.

This book is a Shoal Collective project, edited by Amy Hall, Eliza Egret, Lydia Noon, and Tom Anderson.

Shoal is an independent co-operative of writers and researchers. We produce news articles, investigations, and analysis as a contribution to, and a resource for, movements that are attempting to bring about social and political change.

We also run the Corporate Occupation website, which tracks corporate complicity in Israeli colonisation, militarism, and apartheid.

shoalcollective.org
corporateoccupation.org

Fifty percent of any royalties Shoal Collective receives from the sale of this book will be donated to grass-roots Palestinian organisations and funds chosen by the interviewees.

Dedication

This book is dedicated to Wafa Aludaini, killed alongside her husband Munir when an Israeli air strike hit their home in Deir Al-Balah, central Gaza, in the early hours of September 30, 2024. Her two young children—Balsam, five years old, and Tamin, a seven-month-old baby—were also killed.

Wafa was a journalist and worked in collaboration with the Palestinian-led International Solidarity Movement (ISM). Shoal Collective had been hoping to arrange an interview with Wafa for this book, in the weeks running up to her death.

Like many of the women we interviewed, Wafa was frustrated at the way Gaza was portrayed in the media. So much so that she decided to become a journalist herself, reporting from the frontline of protests, including the Great March of Return, for almost eighteen months, as well as documenting several Israeli attacks on the Gaza Strip.

Wafa was a committed mentor and teacher of Gaza's young people. She led a women's youth group that aimed to change negative stereotypes about Palestinians. She founded the 16th October Media Group, a group of journalists and activists who seek to refocus the world's attention onto the authentic Palestinian narrative. Like so many journalists from Gaza, she was systematically murdered for standing up for what she believed in. May she rest in power.

We would also like to dedicate our work to all of the Palestinian women and girls who have been killed in the anti-colonial struggle against the Israeli occupation, and all the Palestinian women and girls who never asked to be brave.

Shoal Collective, June 2025

Contents

Foreword ix

Introduction 1

INTERVIEWS

Ayah Al-Ghazzawi 4

Lina Nabulsy 11

Samah Fadil 21

Diana Khwaelid 34

Shahd Abusalama 43

Shahd Abusalama (2024 Update) 55

Sireen Khudairy 64

Lama Suleiman 75

Shrouq Aila 85

Rana Abu Rahmah 95

Shatha Abu Srour 101

Ghada Hamdan 115

Mona Al-Farra 122

Mona Al-Farra (2025 Update) 132

Faiza Abu Shamsiyah 141

APPENDICES

Map showing the location of each woman's home in Palestine 152

Events (in chronological order) 153

Places 162

Glossary 169

Palestinian Movements 175

About the Contributors 181

Foreword

By Huwaida Arraf

It is a profound honour to pen the foreword to this second edition of an essential and transformative work. Shoal Collective has created a crucial contribution to our understanding of the Palestinian liberation struggle by centring the voices of Palestinian women—voices that history has too often marginalised or obscured. Amid a struggle defined by occupation, dispossession, genocide, and attempts at whole scale erasure, the stories of Palestinian women showcase a vibrant tapestry of resilience, defiance, and radical thought. These narratives not only challenge mainstream Western perceptions but also redefine what it means to fight for freedom, in all its forms, in the face of extraordinary adversity.

This collection of interviews offers a rare and powerful glimpse into the lived experiences, convictions, and dreams of women who are not merely participants in a broader movement but central architects of resistance. Their voices resound with power and intention, compelling a recentring of the discourse on Palestinian identity, rights, and justice. While titled *Interviews with Radical Palestinian Women*, these women are not 'radical' in the sense of extremism; rather, they embody the enduring spirit of our foremothers—women whose strength, courage, and vision have long been the backbone of our struggle for liberation. Born and raised in the United States, I grew up surrounded by distorted portrayals of Palestinians—and Arabs in general—in Western media. Hollywood's depiction of the submissive, oversexualised, and oppressed Arab woman bore no resemblance to the strong, principled women I knew in my own family, or the countless Palestinian women I encountered during my time organising in occupied Palestine with the International Solidarity Movement.

My paternal grandmother, a legend in the small Galilean village of Mi'ilya, within the Green Line,[1] exemplified this resilience. At nine-months pregnant, she worked the land until labour began, rode her horse home, and gave birth alone. She raised eight children, defended our family's land against Zionist encroachment before, during, and after the Nakba, and remained a cornerstone of her community. Similarly, in my mother's hometown of Beit Sahour, in the West Bank, women led pivotal acts of resistance during the First Intifada, organising boycotts of Israeli goods, spearheading the town's historic tax strike, and sustaining the movement under relentless repression.

Palestinian women's contributions to the national struggle are neither new nor ancillary; they are organic and foundational. From the earliest recorded protest in 1893 against settlement construction in the town of Afula, to the establishment of the Orthodox Aid Society for the Poor in 1903, women have organised to defend land, culture, family, and community. The 1920s saw the creation of the Arab Women's Association and the Palestinian Women's Union, which galvanised women to protest British rule and Zionist colonisation, established mutual aid networks to sustain their communities, and advocated for Palestinian rights at regional and international forums.

This struggle has always been remarkable for its interreligious unity, focusing on shared goals of liberation and dignity. From the First Palestinian Arab Women's Congress in 1929—which brought together over three hundred women from diverse religious and social backgrounds to plan boycotts, protests, lobbying, and media work—to rural women's direct support of resistance fighters in the 1936–39 Palestinian Revolt and beyond.

The Nakba of 1948 brought unprecedented displacement and loss, but Palestinian women's resilience never wavered. Figures such as Hayat Al-Balbisi, who provided medical care to refugees, and Hind Al-Husseini, who founded the Dar Al-Tifl Al-Arabi orphanage, illustrate the enduring spirit of care and defiance that has characterised their response to oppression. These efforts have left lasting legacies, exemplified by institutions like Dar Al-Tifl, which continues to serve Palestinian children today.

1 The 'Green Line', or the 1948 Armistice line, marks the furthest advance of the Zionist forces at that time.

This book is a testament to their legacy. It amplifies voices that demand recognition not as passive victims but as architects of resistance and agents of transformative change. It underscores that the liberation of Palestine is inseparable from the fight for gender justice and that the strength of the movement lies in its diversity and inclusivity.

While figures like Leila Khaled, Hanan Ashrawi, Khalida Jarrar, and Ahed Tamimi are celebrated globally, countless unnamed women have equally stitched the fabric of Palestinian resistance. From educators and caregivers to advocates, activists, and fighters, their sacrifices are born of necessity, resilience, and an unyielding commitment to justice. Their stories, as chronicled here, provide crucial insight into the Palestinian movement's heart and soul.

In a time when understanding the Palestinian struggle has never been more urgent, this book invites readers to explore the unique challenges and triumphs of women engaged in this fight. It is a call to action: to honour the voices within these pages is to renew our commitment to the broader fight against oppression and to amplify the message of freedom, justice, equity, and peace.

May these stories move you not just to solidarity, but to action. May they inspire hope and reaffirm the belief that justice is not only possible, but inevitable.

Ayah Al-Ghazzawi

Samah Fadil

Diana Khwaelid

Shahd Abusalama

Lama Suleiman

Shrouq Aila

Mona Al-Farra

Faiza Abu Shamsiyah

Introduction

Women have always been an essential part of the movement for Palestinian liberation, as protesters, community organisers, in documenting Israel's colonial violence, and in the armed struggle. However, their role is often sidelined or ignored in discussions of the fight for a free Palestine.

As we finalise this edition of *Interviews with Radical Palestinian Women*, Israel has been carrying out genocide in Gaza for nearly two years, since October 2023. In this campaign of devastation, the colonial power has furthered its goal of taking more Palestinian land and erasing tens of thousands of Palestinians, including entire family lineages.

Meanwhile, Israel has begun a deadly offensive in the West Bank, with an alarming increase in air strikes, expelling thousands of Palestinians from refugee camps in the north, and emboldening Israeli settlers, to further minimise any prospect of a 'two-state solution'.

Israel has also attacked Lebanon, Syria, and Iran during this time, creating deeper regional insecurity and once again rendering the concept of the 'rules-based international order' meaningless.

As always, much of the Western media coverage has sought to depoliticise what is happening. Horrific crimes of genocide have, after two years of inaction from world leaders, become normalised. Palestinians are invited only to comment on the humanitarian situation and the horrors they are experiencing, while no space is made for their political agency and experience. Within this, women are often portrayed as passive victims of violence.

Yet many Palestinian women, like those we have interviewed, are not only active in the struggle for the freedom of their people, but in globally connected struggles for liberation—from anarchism and feminism to ecology and disability justice, and against systems of oppression from authoritarianism and white supremacy to patriarchy and capitalism.

The conversations published here took place between 2018 and 2025 and describe experiences of living under occupation, under siege, surviving Israeli genocide, and being part of the Palestinian diaspora. And while they might confront stereotypes associated with women in the Middle East, they do not shy away from the challenges of being a woman within patriarchy. These experiences shape how the women we spoke to see the world as radicals.

In talking about the Palestinian anti-colonial struggle, many of the women critique the authoritarian nature of the Palestinian Authority, and demand a liberation which deals holistically with the many layers of oppression that they face.

We hope that the breadth of topics covered in the interviews will help people outside Palestine to understand that the Palestinian struggle is multidimensional, and to see radical Palestinian women—like Ghada Hamden, a farmer in the West Bank village of Bil'in; Ayah Al-Ghazzawi, a Boycott, Divest and Sanctions (BDS) activist in Gaza; and Shatha Abu Srour, a disability rights advocate in Bethlehem—as allies in our global struggles for freedom rather than passive victims of Israeli state policies.

It's important to note that our experiences as writers and researchers based in Britain have inevitably shaped the questions that we have asked and how we have carried out the work. We bring with us our own interpretation of what it means to be 'radical', which will have had some influence on the finished book. Still, we hope that hearing from Palestinian women themselves will make a useful contribution to strengthening our movements and building international solidarity.

A simple timeline of events and a glossary of terminology are provided at the back of the book.

We owe a huge debt of gratitude to all of the women interviewed for their time and their honesty. They have taken a personal risk by expressing their political views so frankly, and we hope that the book does justice to their courage and strength in the face of oppression.

INTERVIEWS

Ayah Al-Ghazzawi

Ayah is from Gaza City, but was displaced to Khan Yunis during the genocide. She is a Boycott, Divestment and Sanctions (BDS) activist and a member of the One Democratic State Campaign. We interviewed Ayah between December 3, 2024, and January 6, 2025, via WhatsApp voice notes, which she sent whenever she managed to get a strong enough internet connection.

Where are you from in Gaza and where are you living now?
Well, that's a question of history for a Palestinian. I am a Palestinian refugee whose ancestors were ethnically cleansed from the occupied city of Jaffa in 1948. Since the very establishment of Israel, I haven't been able to visit or see it.

I was born and raised in Gaza City. Before the genocide I lived in the heart of Gaza, in a very beautiful place—very vibrant—now it's classified as northern Gaza by the occupation. When the genocide started we were forced to evacuate our home and we came to southern Gaza. I was displaced many times. First I was displaced to Khan Yunis and then to Rafah and now back to Khan Yunis, in a tent which is not very comfortable, but that's all I've got at the moment.

Do you come from a political family?
Actually on the contrary, my family and I don't have anything to do with politics. But, the thing is, we're born into a political situation. You find yourself in a political situation when you are also in a colonial context. You find your lands are taken away from you. I belong to my ancestors who were evicted, uprooted, and ethnically cleansed from their hometowns back in 1948. I don't have access to my native

town while Jewish people from all over the world can come and live in Palestine, even if their ancestors were never in Palestine. The irony! I don't have the same right, my family and others don't have the same right, no Palestinians have the same right. That's not only part of colonisation but an apartheid regime.

So back to your question—my family has no political background. I don't have a political background. We are a very peaceful family, we seek education, we seek personal growth and professional development. We try to build a life at a time where it's completely complicated and hard to get a good life.

Do you remember when you first wanted to take part in activism and why?

As I said before, we as Palestinians are born into a political situation, so when I was little I wondered what I could do for my people, for my cause, to get rid of the coloniser—what could I do to be free, to have a dignified life? I was considering what was happening on the ground, but I didn't have enough knowledge. I didn't have solutions or answers, they were just the questions boggling in my mind, until I started university.

At university we studied literary criticism, we studied novels which tackled stories from colonised people and we projected that onto our reality. We were also talking about international law and our rights as an occupied people, so this cultivated my vision. It culminated in one thing: to engage in a peaceful way to help my people. And there comes the role of BDS. I first learned about BDS from university, from lecturers and some friends who were volunteers in the movement. I saw that the BDS movement is a very peaceful, very effective way to resist.

I remembered Mahatma Gandhi's experience in India, Nelson Mandela in South Africa, and history teaches us a lot. I thought that this is the right way for me to do something for my sake, for my family, for my people, for my cause—instead of just standing aside with my arms folded and not knowing what to do. I felt like this could make a real change, a real difference. And because BDS discusses Palestinian rights in the light of international law, it's completely legitimate, it's effective and there are results. Many companies who profited from the Israeli system have withdrawn their support for Israel, so that is really amazing.

Another thing is that BDS not only works on decolonisation of the land, but also decolonisation of the mind—which goes hand in hand. It also has a progressive view of women's roles, and I like that about the movement.

How have things changed for you and your family since October 2023?
I think that this is a very important, multidimensional question to all Palestinians in Gaza because we lost our basic right of a dignified life, we lost the feeling of safety and we have been segregated—northern Gaza is segregated from southern Gaza. We can't get access to our homes in the north, we don't have the capability to see our cousins or friends who are still there, and we became displaced many times. I myself have been displaced at least three times—every time I try to settle in a place, Israel comes and forcibly evicts us and destroys every means of life. Our children have been terrorised, we all have been traumatised.

Before the genocide we did not have a normal life; it was a semi-normal life. It was not enough for us because Israel as a settler-colonial entity established conditions for the colonised, the oppressed Palestinians, not to be able to build a good life, a decent life. It can take a lifetime for a person in Gaza to buy a home, to get married, to have children and all, and then comes Israel in the blink of an eye and takes all this away from you, and that's extremely painful.

Our lives have also been on hold for almost a year and three months now—all this time has been wasted. Before the genocide we had things to do. I work as an English-language teacher in a school and since the beginning of the genocide I did not go to work because schools were targeted. Most of them are not good places now to administer education and what is left of them is inhabited by people who have lost their homes. We don't have shelters like Israelis do, so they have become places for homeless Palestinians.

I come from a family where all of our siblings are about the same age and we were just blossoming. I have a dentist brother, and an engineer brother who is taking another speciality in business administration and IT. He started that before the genocide but now he's two years behind, he's not moving forward. I also have a sister in university who also lost a year and a few months. She can't attend the classes. My siblings who are still in universities and schools don't have devices, don't have stable internet connections for schooling. One sibling is in secondary school, in her last year. She was supposed to be done the year of the genocide and she is now supposed to be in her first year of college but none of this happened. So you can see that life has been on hold, our time has been wasted.

I had a dream of pursuing a master's degree in postcolonial literature and now I can't. I tried to apply for a scholarship during the genocide and I was not able to go forward to the second stage. I contacted a friend, who is very excellent, who applied for the same scholarship and she got rejected too. We found out that it is because we are stuck in Gaza and the crossing is still closed.

When the crossing was open during the genocide there were fees [to leave Gaza via the Rafah crossing], coordination fees they're called, but they were so extravagant, so expensive. One had to pay $5,000 for each adult, and $2,500 dollars for children who were under sixteen years old.

Now instead of being in our warm beds, in our safe homes, we are in tents. Believe me when I say there is no kind of privacy whatsoever. We also don't have access to healthy food. Vegetables are very expensive, fruits also are even more expensive than vegetables, there are no sources of income and there is no healthcare.

We are displaced and homeless. I lost my apartment. I am a new bride and I had lived in my apartment for only about four months before the genocide. It was brand new, everything in it was new: the furniture, my clothes, the kitchen things. I didn't have the time to enjoy them. The house was blown up. My apartment was one storey of a building that belonged to my father-in-law—it's a three-storey building—and the whole building was blown up so we have no home now and we are displaced and homeless, thanks to Israel.

How have people in Gaza been organising to support each other during this time?

Palestinians who have vehicles help in transferring the wounded people, the martyrs, to hospitals to get treatment. They give blankets, they give mattresses to those who lost everything, so this is one of the things that we can see, we can touch; it's tangible.

At the beginning of the genocide, people tried to support each other in whatever way they could, whether it was giving shelter to those who had lost their homes or were forcibly evicted; or to provide water to places that didn't have water; or to give food; or even by good word—to extend condolences to people who lost dear ones. But after some time of the genocide, everyone has become drained. They lost the things they could offer to other people. Everyone has become busy with their own selves, with their own families, with their own loved ones. And because Israel created a situation where people are overcrowded, there's no privacy and not enough space for each family. So you find that people, after some time, begin fighting and bickering.

I think this is a very bad effect of the genocide, that Israel hit the social structure of the Palestinian people in Gaza. Generally speaking, the Palestinian people are fairly co-operative, very supportive, very affectionate. We feel for each other because we are all in the same boat, we are suffering from the same occupier, coloniser, and we know that the solution is to stick together. But again Israel has made sure that it has created a situation where the Palestinian people have just had enough. At the same time, they are drained, exhausted, they are stripped of everything they can use, not just to save other people but also to save themselves.

Is there a lot of support in Gaza for BDS and do people see it as an effective tactic?

I must say that it's very challenging in Gaza to endorse the Boycott, Divestment and Sanctions movement. It's because Gaza and the West Bank are the second biggest market for Israel, keeping in mind that Israel is a colonial state and occupier and it has all the power. This is because we have the Oslo Accords and there is a part of it about economics, but also because Israel has been besieging Gaza since 2006.[1] It destroys factories and it paralyses the economy so we are not empowered enough to produce our own goods—we are dependent more on what we import from outside. Some of the goods are from Egypt, from Turkey, from Jordan, but the largest part comes from Israel.

1 In the words of the Institute for Middle East Understanding: 'The economic arrangements set out under the [1990s] Oslo Accords, particularly the Paris Protocol, and Israel's restrictions on Palestinian movement and development first imposed under Oslo, have devastated the Palestinian economy, which has become largely dependent on international aid and the transfer of Palestinian tax money collected by Israel.' See IMEU, 'Explainer: The Oslo Accords', September 1, 2023, https://imeu.org/article/explainer-the-oslo-accords.

It creates a stereotype, an image, in the minds of Palestinians in Gaza, and in the West Bank, that the quality of Israeli goods is much better than any other, and that it is superior in everything and that's why all people have to consume Israeli goods. So that's why when we talk about BDS, we talk about decolonising the mind; we have to break the stereotype.

But we notice that there is a growing culture [of support for BDS], especially among the educated elite coming out from schools and universities. There is the hope of the volunteers who are staunch supporters of the BDS movement and who keep talking about BDS everywhere, whether in schools, in clubs, on the streets. We go to markets—we try to convince the owners of the market stalls not to bring Israeli goods because 16 percent of the fees of the Israeli goods goes to the Israeli army, which uses the money to buy more weapons, more bullets, more F-16s to kill us.[2] So the answer is, it is very challenging, but there is a hope.

Where do you think international BDS activists should be focusing their efforts at this time?

I think there is a wider scope outside of Palestine to work on BDS. The most important thing nowadays regarding the genocide is to impose sanctions on the weapons manufacturers. Also to pressure governments to cut contracts with Israel and to stop providing Israel with weapons. At the end of the day, we are on the receiving end of those weapons. Israel uses those weapons against Palestinians. So I think that BDS supporters and activists should ask to impose a military embargo on Israel and to demonstrate in front of weapons manufacturers and factories. Also to ask their governments to stop sending their taxes away to Israel in the shape of aid.

I know that there are other companies working in the food industry, for example, McDonald's, Pepsi, Coca-Cola, these are factories that support Israel with money, with sponsoring teams, etc. I think we all need to ask these companies to stop supporting Israel and to withdraw profits from Israeli branches. This money is used in killing

2 Yael Marom and Jessica Devaney, 'Bringing the Boycott Back Home: Palestinian Stores Drop Israeli Goods', +972 *Magazine*, September 3, 2014, https://www.972mag.com/bringing-the-boycott-back-home-palestinian-stores-drop-israeli-goods.

more Palestinians and the Palestinian blood is on the hands of all those who profit from the Israeli multi-tiered system of oppression that is occupation, settler colonialism, and apartheid.

You're a member of the One Democratic State campaign. How hopeful are you of that goal in the midst of Israel's ongoing genocide and ethnic cleansing campaign?

I've been a member since 2019 and I adopted this vision because I see it as a comprehensive liberation project that can be a substitute for all the so-called solutions, for example, the two-state solution.

I think that Israel has changed the demographics of Palestine by bringing waves of millions of Jews, from across the globe, to give a Jewish identity to the Palestinian land and territories. It has created a situation where it is very difficult to bring, for example, those Jewish people back to their countries. But it also brought a generation who were born or brought up in the occupied Palestinian territories, known as Israel now, and they have no say in what Israel has committed against Palestinians. They did not choose to be in Palestine, they were just brought here or born into a political situation, just like us. Of course, with the crucial difference that our ancestors have always been in Palestine, we have always been in Palestine, unlike them. So I think it is a generosity of Palestinians—decolonised people—to call for a one democratic state for all inhabitants of Palestine—Jewish people, Arabs, Christians, everyone to live in equality or on the same foot of freedom, equality, and dignity. That is a generosity of Palestinians, to say the least.

Also I think it is a very rational solution to getting rid of Israel, of the Zionist mentality, because it was created in the Middle East to cause trouble for everyone and to serve the interests of colonial powers. In the past it was Britain which helped in establishing Israel through the Balfour Declaration, and today it is the US, the biggest superpower and the sole biggest power in the world.[3] So I am hopeful, very much hopeful, that one democratic state will be endorsed over time by everyone because it is a just solution for everyone. It's a win-win. You see my point?

---

3 A statement made by the British foreign secretary, Arthur Balfour, in 1917, which was the green light for the international Zionist movement to begin its attempts to colonise Palestine in earnest. See the glossary for more information.

Lina Nabulsy

Lina Nabulsy (a pseudonym) is from Bethlehem in the West Bank. Lina is a political organiser, active in the struggle against the Israeli occupation, and a critic of the Palestinian Authority. We interviewed Lina in July 2018, in a restaurant in Bethlehem.

Can you tell us about how you were first politicised?
I just woke up one day and there was an occupation, there were soldiers on the streets. I grew up with the occupation. My mum tried to protect me and my sisters, to make sure that we didn't get into politics, but it didn't work.

During the Second Intifada [which began in 2000], things started to become clearer to me. Before that I was trying to understand what was going on. I still had a glimmer of hope and it was the era of the Oslo 'peace process'. After Oslo, when they started putting checkpoints in our town, I saw that something was really wrong.

During the Intifada I went to throw rocks at the Israeli soldiers. But I was never a good aim and I ended up hitting the *shebab* [the other demonstrators]. So instead, I helped by carrying buckets of rocks to the frontlines. At that time I was arrested and beaten by the Israelis. I had just turned sixteen. I was grabbed by a plain-clothes police officer and then Special Forces beat the shit out of me with batons—I was pinned on the floor for half an hour. Afterwards, I was traumatised.

They couldn't hold me because I was underage and covered in bruises. Instead, they made me sign a piece of paper to say that I wouldn't complain that I had been beaten up. I was given conditions not to be in the vicinity of Jerusalem. Later on, I got more involved in student political organising.

What was it like to be a female organiser during the Second Intifada?

At that time the space was more open for women than it is now. Society has become much more conservative since. There has been so much killing and death that religion becomes the only thing that people can hold onto. As a woman, you have to do everything that a man does, and more, to get accepted. I would usually be called the 'sister of the men', or that I was 'as strong as a man'. You have to be manly for them to respect you. I had to be strong in front of people.

But because of women's place in the struggle against the Israeli occupation, we were given much more freedom than in other places. Because of that, women are better off here than in other Arab countries.

Can you tell us about the effect of the 2011 Middle Eastern and North African uprisings in Palestine?

The revolutions happening in the Arab world awakened the desire in Palestine to stand up and shout. Palestinian women felt that this was our time to scream too.

During the Second Intifada the streets had been our space and we did what we wanted. But during the uprisings in Tunisia and Egypt, we got a wake-up call that the Palestinian Authority (PA) was against us. During the Tahrir Square protests in Egypt, the Palestinian police began stopping us in Ramallah [a city in the West Bank], asking to see our permits. They started to increase the pressure on us, and I became more aware of the role of the PA. We had forgotten how the PA, and the system itself, had been transformed since Arafat. The institutionalisation of capitalism began after [the death of Yasser] Arafat. Arafat was still a revolutionary. He never took off his revolutionary clothes.

Nothing was institutionalised and he was paying people in suitcases full of cash. There was still a sense of revolution. Arafat had an iron fist against his opponents, but it was nothing compared to Abu Mazen [Mahmoud Abbas]. They [the US] brought Salam Fayyad to power, that World Bank motherfucker, and his mandate was to basically end 'corruption' and create institutions.[1]

1 Salam Fayyad was prime minister of the Palestinian Authority between 2007 and 2013. He had previously worked for the IMF and World Bank. Fayyad's career in the PA had been strongly backed by the US and EU.

Then we started seeing that more and more of the government budget was going towards 'security'. I realised that police were getting trained to fight against their own people. Soldiers were getting trained in protest dispersal. Our security forces were being trained by Americans and Europeans.

The influx of loans began. Everyone with a car in Ramallah has had a loan, which means people are tied to the system now. European funding has destroyed the essence of the Palestinian grass roots. We used to have Popular Committees that would cooperate with each other. We didn't rely on the mercy of the US and Europe. But now we are slaves to government funding. If the US decides tomorrow to stop funding the PA, then it will be shattered in a few months. This was the work of Fayyad.

Can you tell us about women's role in the anti-PA demonstrations in Palestine since the Middle Eastern and North African uprisings of 2011?

I feel that after the March 15, 2011, protests against the Palestinian Authority, we reclaimed a space for women that had been missing since the Second Intifada. We started having debates as activists—what kind of liberation do we want? I remember thinking, if this is what I am going to get then I don't want it. I don't want to fight for another capitalist form of a colony. I don't want the democracy that they're talking about. I don't want an Arab state like Egypt. I don't want to live in a place where I'm not free as a woman. We started to ask a lot of questions like this. It's not just about ending the occupation. It's much more global than that.

During the 2011 protests, both Hamas in Gaza, and Fatah here in the West Bank, did everything they could to destroy our movement. Here in Ramallah, the protests got crushed by the PA. They targeted us and went after us individually, isolating us from each other. There was coordination between the Palestinian and Israeli security forces to get activists. [Later on] my friend Basil Al Araj was tortured by the PA, and then released so that the Israelis could assassinate him.[2]

---

2 Basil Al Araj was a well-known youth organiser and writer from the village of Al Walaja, committed to reigniting the struggle for the liberation of Palestine. He was imprisoned by the PA for six months in 2016 with five of his comrades. PA president Mahmoud Abbas boasted at the time that their arrest was an example of PA-Israeli co-operation.

Female activists involved in the movement were branded as 'whores on the streets of the headquarters of the president'.

When I was arrested and taken into custody by the PA, I saw people bleeding, being tortured. You get tortured first in the Palestinian prisons, and then your forced confessions get used by the Israelis. Often, you get released from the Palestinian jail, then soon after you are arrested by the Israelis. There is coordination between them through the DCO [District Coordinating Office—an institution created during the Oslo agreements].

Torture is legal in Israel.[3] But in Israel you wouldn't get tortured badly for a comment you made on Facebook. You wouldn't get whipped or hung from your feet.

If we get rid of the occupation tomorrow then our next target should be the Palestinian Authority.

The six men were held without charge by the PA, and only released after a hunger strike. Four of Basil's comrades were soon detained by Israeli forces and held without charge in administrative detention. Basil went underground for a year, but was killed after a gunfight with Israeli soldiers in 2017.

See Charlotte Silver, 'Why Is Mahmoud Abbas Boasting of Jailing Palestine's Youth?' *Electronic Intifada*, September 1, 2016, https://electronicintifada.net/blogs/charlotte-silver/why-mahmoud-abbas-boasting-jailing-palestines-youth; and 'Thousands of Palestinians Join Funeral of Resistance for Basil al-Araj', *Samidoun*, March 19, 2017, https://samidoun.net/2017/03/thousands-of-palestinians-join-funeral-of-resistance-for-basil-al-araj.

3 Torture was completely legal and widespread in Israeli custody from the start of the occupation. The use of torture was limited somewhat in 1999. Israeli human rights group B'Tselem writes:

> In September 1999, following a series of petitions filed by human rights organizations and by Palestinians interrogated by the ISA [the Israel Security Agency], Israel's High Court of Justice (HCJ) ruled that Israeli law does not empower ISA interrogators to use physical means in interrogation. The justices ruled that the specific methods discussed in the petitions—including painful binding, shaking, placing a sack on a person's head for prolonged periods of time and sleep deprivation—were unlawful. However, they also held that ISA agents who exceed their authority and use 'physical pressure' may not necessarily bear criminal responsibility for their actions, if they are later found to have used these methods in a 'ticking bomb' case, based on the 'necessity defense'. Following this ruling, reports of torture and ill-treatment in ISA interrogations did drop. However, ISA agents continued to use interrogation methods that constitute abuse and even torture, relying on the court's recognition of the 'ticking bomb' exception. These methods were not limited to exceptional cases and quickly became standard interrogation policy.

See 'Torture and Abuse in Interrogation', B'Tselem, November 11, 2017, https://www.btselem.org/torture. These modest limits on the use of torture in Israeli custody create an added incentive for Israel to outsource the torture of Palestinian prisoners to the PA.

What happened to the protesters in Gaza?

The protesters in Gaza were calling for the same things as us. And they were crushed too, by Hamas. In Gaza they are suffocated. Hamas knows who you are, they know your family.

And what about the summer 2018 protests?

After 2011, the protests continued against the PA's policies and they grew, leading up to what's happening now. The [anti-PA] demonstration in Ramallah in 2018 was considered a big protest. The demands were for an end to the sanctions on Gaza. It's very difficult to believe that the PA is participating openly in the siege of Gaza and they have no shame in saying that they're blocking the salaries of the people in Gaza—salaries that are coming from outside, from the EU and Arab states.

The PA are also letting people die. They have stopped medical transfers of patients between the West Bank and Gaza.

The repression of the protest was a show of force. To show us what they can do. It's a little taste of what would happen if people dare to continue to shout, and to say *no*. The violence didn't come as a shock for me, but for other people it was a surprise. Protesters were beaten, electric-shock batons were used on the street. The PA used tear gas, stun grenades. All of them are weapons that the Israelis use on us too. Forty people were arrested on that day. Many people who are from Fatah, and are deeply connected with the PA, knew it was wrong. But the security forces are the ones running the show.

The best scenario for the Israelis is to have a Palestinian security force strong enough to maintain the situation as it is. That's what the security forces have been brainwashed for over the last ten years.

Is there any democracy in the West Bank?

There are no elections, so we don't have any form of choice. The last election was in 2006. What Abbas did [in ousting Hamas from the West Bank in 2007] was not called a coup in the public narrative. But the reality is that he is a dictator who completely took over the authority, and kicked out his Hamas opponents that won an election fair and square.

There isn't any elected body that's currently in control of anything in the PA. It's run fully dictatorship-style, with the president who makes the decisions. The prime minister takes unilateral decisions as well. The three heads of security forces are the people that run the show—the head of intelligence, the head of the preventative security forces, and the people who are in coordination with the Israelis—the DCO. Israel needs this situation to keep us under control. The most important person for both the Americans and the Israelis is the person who controls the PA's security forces.

How should people outside Palestine view the Palestinian Authority?
The PA is more destructive for the struggle right now than anything else. They try to destroy the BDS [Boycott, Divestment and Sanctions] movement. They put on gala events instead of fighting for human rights, and they're hopeless at everything.

People internationally should put the same pressure on the PA as they do the Israeli government. If people want to end injustice, then we must also end the injustice of the PA. It doesn't matter if it's an Israeli or Palestinian soldier beating you, the results are the same.

Can you talk more about European funding?
When it comes to funding, everybody talks about sustainability and democracy, and they come here and give workshops to the 'natives' about the joy of democracy and gender equality. These are good topics if you're talking in luxurious Switzerland. But here the women are kept down by many layers of oppression.

The funders don't deal with the occupation. For example, they talk about the problem of water but they work around the occupation and they won't talk about the core problem, which is that Israel steals our water. The EU gives caravans to the people of the Jordan Valley, and then when the Israelis come and bulldoze them there is no political will to do anything about it. Fuck them and their caravans!

People censor themselves in their grant applications so that they get the funding. Instead of catering to what people need, it's catering to what the white man says we need. If you call for BDS then you aren't going to get funding. With the American funders you have to sign an 'anti-terror' clause before you even receive a grant. You have to submit to torture in order to get the carrot. It's a system of control. And we are losing the essence of what these organisations should be working for. It has created a bubble of very rich NGO workers, both foreign and Palestinian. A class of rich people in Ramallah, pretending to give aid.

I have never seen the gap between the poor and the middle class as big as it is now. There are women in the streets begging for money. But the main recipient of outside funding is the PA. And it is used for training security who throw tear gas at protesters. Israeli soldiers raid our cities each night, but the PA does not stop them. If our soldiers and police can't protect the people then why are they here?

The moment Israeli jeeps arrive in Palestinian territory, all Palestinian police and security are under orders to retreat to their buildings. They're not allowed on the streets. The only reason the Palestinian police are here is to maintain the occupation. The scary thing is that these people working for the PA security forces are our neighbours.

For the PA to be completely in control, they need to control the camps to break the autonomy of the people who live there. They have used many different tactics to do this. Before the creation of the Palestinian Authority, the camps were where the leadership of the fighters would come from. During the Second Intifada [after the PA had been created during the Oslo period], people in the refugee camps were still fighting. And today, the weapons are still in the refugee camps.

The PA has 'combined committees', which are responsible for 'fighting the outlaws' [i.e., the autonomous people still resisting in the camps] in different areas. They have tried to dehumanise the people too. The reputation of the people who live in the refugee camps has changed from 'the glorious fighters', 'the revolutionaries', to 'outlaws'. Unemployment rates have gone crazy in the camps because there's a stigma about employing people living in them.

The Palestinian Authority security forces go into the camps and do raids. They try to get people, but if they can't do it the Israelis do. The level of aggression against people in the refugee camps is one hundred times more than what other West Bank Palestinians face. The majority of people arrested and beaten are from Fatah; they are painted as supporters of Dahlan, Abbas's rival.[4] But many of them are not.

4 Mohammed Dahlan is a former member of the Central Committee of Fatah, and a former PA head of preventative security. He was expelled from Fatah in 2011 and has since been accused of poisoning Yasser Arafat. He is still influential on Palestinian politics from his home in exile in the UAE. See, for example, Ramzy Baroud, 'Mahmoud Abbas

Can you explain about the co-option of resistance by the PA?
The Popular Struggle Coordination Committee (PSCC) and the Ministry of Resistance to the Wall and Colonies are both instruments of the PA.[5] Grass-roots activists tried to get involved, but the PA has basically been more destructive to the non-violent resistance than anything else. They got corrupted by money. Where does this money evaporate to?

How do you feel about the BDS movement?
BDS is the most important thing for me. I would love to see things move from the inside out. It's very difficult for us inside [Palestine] to change things. We can only beat them with resilience, and fight for our values within a society that's collapsing. To fight for love and for good.

I am fighting to keep what I love in Palestine. I'm fighting for freedom, for equality between people. Fighting to maintain myself morally. The struggle is global and not local. When we need to scream 'stop', we do. But for people outside Palestine there is more freedom for people to shout, more freedom for people to put pressure on Israel, to call for boycotts. Israel is trying hard to stop BDS. They're using all their might to fight BDS internally and externally.

There are so many moral reasons to fight Israel beyond justice for Palestine. The same weapons used against us in Palestine will be soon used against our comrades in Europe. The space is shrinking everywhere around the world for speaking out. If we don't fight then we don't have a chance to survive the storms that are ahead.

Can you tell us a bit about what motivates you to go on struggling?
For me the struggle is the same here in Palestine as for the Black Panthers. We are fighting one evil in this world. The thing that makes

---

vs Mohammed Dahlan: The Showdown Begins', *Mondoweiss*, March 31, 2014, https://mondoweiss.net/2014/03/mahmoud-mohammed-showdown.

5 The Popular Struggle Coordination Committee (PSCC) is an umbrella body of representatives of the grass-roots Popular Resistance Committees. Many Palestinians, however, see the PSCC as an undemocratic body, set up to bring the popular resistance in line with the aims of Fatah and the PA.

The Ministry of Resistance to the Wall and Colonies is part of the Palestinian Authority. It has played a direct role in popular resistance. For example, during the 2018 struggle against the demolition of the village of Khan Al Ahmar, the ministry paid for buses to the protests and provided food to those resisting the evictions. Many Palestinians critiqued the ministry for monopolising the resistance and dominating the narrative.

me a revolutionary is injustice. We draw inspiration from freedom movements from around the world. Black Lives Matter is something that is close to my heart. The Zapatista movement [in Mexico], and watching the women rise up in Egypt and in Syria makes me stand stronger.

Our struggle has to be global. A struggle against capitalism and against patriarchy. Women need to be in charge. Men have destroyed everything. Those that create life are the ones enslaved, and are not in power. The only way is for women globally to take over completely in all aspects of life. But not women like Theresa May [former British prime minister], Hillary Clinton [US politician], or Ayelet Shaked [Israeli politician].

Good men should support us as we're fighting together for a free world. But the struggle has to be led by women.

What kind of world would you like to see?

For Palestine, and all around the world, I would like to see a place where we're allowed to live life. I want a completely different world. I want liberation. A world where respect is returned to humanity in all forms and colours. Where people are allowed to be who they are without living in fear.

I don't care what they label this place. I don't care about flags. I want freedom without nationality and identity, not the communist type or the Islamic type. I want a place where everyone of any religion is respected. Animals have to be free as well. I want utopia and I won't accept anything less.

If we die in the process of fighting for this world, then at least we have died fighting the good fight. The moment we stop believing we can get to this utopia, then we don't have anything left to fight for. Why would you take another breath if you didn't believe anything can change?

Governments kill our hopes. They make us live like rats in offices, digging in holes and searching for money. Part of the way they destroy us is to take away our hopes. But the reality is that miracles happen every day. People need to realise that there is nothing left, no hope for our children, if we don't fight. The planet is screaming, 'Enough, I'm done'. Soon the water will disappear here, and we will all be fighting in this region for water. Nature has been occupied and killed.

Maybe when people feel desperate enough, we will move together globally. Why not have global protests shouting that we've had enough. Scream '*khalas*!' [enough]. If I can't live a dignified life, it's not worth living.

Armies live in fear. If you eliminate the fear then the soldiers will turn around and join us. The idea that we are all one can eliminate that fear. And if one of us is still in prison, then none of us are free.

Samah Fadil

Samah lives in Tiohtià:ke/Montreal, Canada. She is an Afro-Palestinian writer, poet, editor, and translator. Her parents left Gaza with her eldest sibling before she was born and the family lived in several different countries before settling in Canada when she was a child. We interviewed Samah in September 2024, via an online video call.

Do you remember when you became politically active or awakened? What was the inspiration?

I don't know that there was one specific moment that made me politically aware; it was probably a series of events and observations that I had when I was younger.

Both my parents are Palestinian, so already I was a bit more politically aware than the average kid in the 1990s. My father is a Black Palestinian. So those intersectionalities—before I even knew what intersectionality was—meant that I was aware of certain things that my friends around me weren't necessarily aware of. Plus, my parents were so politically aware because of their Palestinianness. My father was really into politics so he had the news on all the time. That was the background noise of my childhood: the news, and of course the news in Arabic. A lot of it covered things that were happening in Palestine, or in the Middle East in general, from a completely different perspective to the way it was reported here in the West. Seeing how it was reported in Arabic versus how it was reported in English versus how it was reported in French—because I live in Quebec—was totally different. That made me aware that politics were at play and I asked myself, 'Why is this being reported in such a different way, whether it's here or there?'

That's what made me want to go into journalism. I wanted to understand why we are being portrayed in such a way? Why is it that Black people are portrayed in a certain way? Why is it that people who look like me or have the same faith or religious beliefs, why are we portrayed in a certain way? So all of this was circling around in my mind during recess while the other kids were playing [laughs].

I guess if I had to choose one moment, or one visual that stuck with me, it was in 2000, at the time of the Second Intifada in Gaza. There were reels coming out of a little boy, Muhammad al-Durrah, who was being sheltered by his father [under his father's arm]. I think he was twelve years old. His father was pleading with the Israeli army to stop shooting and then they shot his kid on live TV. Muhammad was around my age and it really stayed with me—just how casual it was, how careless it was. His life had no value to the soldiers. And then, the year after that 9/11 happened, and, let's just say that made me painfully aware of my identity.

Your parents were forced from Jaffa to Gaza during the Nakba and then left Gaza before you were born. How did they instil a sense of Palestinian identity in you and your siblings and how did they keep it going after you moved to Canada?

Before we moved to Canada as refugees, my family lived in Kuwait and the United Arab Emirates. It was way easier to visit Palestine back then, so they would go back and visit family almost every year before I was born. I didn't have that experience unfortunately, but my older siblings were instilled with a Palestinian identity because they were able to connect with cousins, aunties, and uncles. Once we moved to Canada it became much harder. It was more expensive and then with the rising tensions it was almost impossible, but I did still have the opportunity to go.

My parents were born and raised in Palestine, so you can take them out of Palestine but you can't take Palestine out of them. So growing up, looking back, I see that all the food we had, all the art on the walls, the big poster of the golden dome [the Al-Aqsa mosque in Al-Quds/ Jerusalem], the news, the shows, the dialect—it was all Palestinian.

When I talk to someone who's Lebanese, or Syrian, they ask, 'Are you Palestinian?' My parents were not trying to hide where we came from or that we were Palestinian. My mother reminded us very clearly that we are from Jaffa, we were exiled to Gaza. We lived in Gaza but we're not from Gaza in a way that, when I was young, I didn't quite understand. As I grew older I saw why she was so specific.

How often have you been able to go back to Palestine?
I've been twice that I remember. It's funny because a year or two ago I actually saw a photo of my family in Gaza in the early 1990s, I saw my little face in the back and I'm like 'oh, that's me!' 1999 was the last time I went, right before the Second Intifada. I was really lucky to be able to go and hang out with all of my cousins. I cherish the times that I was able to go and meet both my grandmothers—my grandfathers unfortunately passed before I was born. Hopefully it's not the last time. I will get the opportunity to go and visit once again, that's my belief.

You've written powerfully about how you have learned more about your family history over the years. Can you explain more about that process, has it changed how you see yourself?
I've been writing since I was a child, before I realised that it could be a career perhaps. But I always wrote with a really big blind spot in my life. There's so much I didn't know about my background and the specific experience that we went through, beyond us being Palestinian and having to flee because we were targeted by Israeli soldiers, like most Palestinians.

Unfortunately, I only started really learning about this history after my father passed away in 2016, my grandmother passed away a month later. That's when my own family back home started opening up to me about my father back in the day, how he was, why he left, what his responsibility was towards the family as the eldest son. Hearing all of this stuff from my aunts reignited this need in me to transcribe everything.

My father was very silent—he didn't talk about hardships. You know Black men, they don't really talk about that; it's like pulling teeth. I learned that my grandmother also was like that, that she was never emotional, she was very like 'This has to be done, what's emotion got to do with it? No time to dwell on the past.' That's one thing she said when I went to Gaza: 'The past is dead so don't dwell on it.'

Now that I'm older I don't necessarily agree with that sentiment. I understand why she had to say it to me for self-preservation, but once I started learning all of that stuff from my aunt I was upset because I was like, 'Why didn't I know all of this?' But it sparked in me this idea that I have to write it down because I don't want it to be lost. And from there it reignited this need to just write, whether it's creative, about my family history, or poetry that reimagines my family history, whichever it is it just needs to be transcribed. And that's not to take away from the oral history—we have a really rich oral history in Palestine—but my grandmother didn't learn how to read and write for me not to write our history down.

It seems that the women in your family have had a big influence on you. Can you say a bit more about that?

The women in my family have always been very strong. My mum's opinion was as important as my dad's, she was always very honest, there was no fear of it not being equal between my parents. My grandmother on my father's side, she was the matriarch of my family. In Palestine, families often live in the same building so it's the grandmother, the grandfather, the aunts and all that. My grandmother was on the top floor and she had her house in order.

When I went to Gaza as a kid I was shocked. It was the first time I met my aunts. They were loud, funny, and independent, smoking their shisha—totally the opposite of what I saw portrayed on TV of Palestinian, Arab, or Black women. My aunts were unambiguously dark-skinned Black women who were independent, super funny, and were afraid of no man. One of my aunts never married, two of my aunts never had kids. You usually hear, 'Oh, Muslim Arab women, they get married, have kids, they're obedient, subservient, blah blah', so when I met them, it totally shattered what I was told to believe by Western media and I wanted to be like them. I'm really happy that I had that experience.

Even my older sisters were like this beacon for me because they were always challenging—challenging the status quo, challenging my parents with their ideas, their politics and everything—it really inspired me. I'm the culmination of all of those things, all of these women and the fact that my father always told me to speak my mind and say what you gotta say, just know how to back it up.

I didn't appreciate it as much when I was a kid, but now I know I wouldn't be as outspoken as I am if my sisters hadn't taken a chance back in the day. I exist within the context—within their context.

You still have family back in Gaza, what kind of challenges have they been facing since Israel began its genocidal assault?
You said it. Literally they're facing genocide. I don't think there's anything that can supersede that. We come from Gaza City which is more in the north, it was one of the first places that was evacuated and they've been moving ever since. Part of my family was able to evacuate to Egypt. I have one family member who was able to evacuate to Qatar, my cousin who is in a band. My aunts, who are elderly now, they're still in Gaza. It's really been difficult because we raised the money to get one of my aunts on the evacuation list and the next day Israel closed the Rafah crossing [to Egypt], so she's still in Gaza right now, in a tent.

But you try to ask them how's it going, how we can help, and they always say 'we're good, we're okay'. It's not that they're used to it, but it's a resilience—I can't even imagine what it takes. I complain when it's raining outside. It really puts things in perspective but right now they're managing. They're extremely resourceful, you wouldn't believe the type of things they can come up with, with what they have. And that was before October 7, they've had to deal with that for a really long time, especially since there's been a blockade on Gaza. All the resources they had were so limited. So they had a kind of training before this phase right now. This phase is unimaginable but they're surviving and of course there are some who have not.

I have family members who were murdered—as far as we know there were eight members of my family on my mum's side who were murdered. I never met them but I still mourn them and I still grieve what could have been, and the relationship that I could have had if it wasn't for the Zionist state. All of these relationships and moments that were robbed from Palestinians, simply due to the fact that they were Palestinians. Israel wants so badly to separate, displace, and erase us. It's tough but I don't have time to process.

What has solidarity with Gaza been like from Canada?
Well, if you're talking about Canada as the settler colonial state, then shit. Really bad. They've put all their chips into supporting Israel, which is not surprising. If you're talking about the people though, then the people have been great. There has been a lot of organising and protesting around what Canada has chosen to do, a lot of following

Justin Trudeau wherever he goes and making sure he remembers that he's aiding and abetting genocide. So the people have been organising.

Again, they were organising way before October 7, but since then they have not stopped and so many people are showing up and showing out. They go almost monthly all the way to Ottawa [from Montreal], which is a few hours' drive, to go to the Parliament and protest in front of the government. Specifically the Arabs and Muslims in Montreal, and in other places, have really been showing up and showing out, protesting and boycotting the places that need to be boycotted. It's been really good to see that they haven't let up. We'll always be here but our government won't.

How do you see the connections between the settler colonialism of Canada and the settler colonialism of Israel?
I don't see a difference. And it really makes me feel ... it irks me inside that for me to live comfortably here somebody somewhere had to suffer. Whether twenty years ago or two hundred years ago somebody had to suffer and lose a part of their land for me to be here and that's just the reality of it. I'm somebody who had to come here as a refugee because our land was taken, and I have nowhere else to go. It's just a cycle, and right now what we're seeing in Palestine is down to the same [settler colonial] machine—it's what created Canada. What's unique about the current genocide is that it's broadcast 24/7 onto our screens and the Israeli military is using new weapons and new types of warfare that we haven't seen before. The methods and the goals though are the same as any other settler colonial state—whether it be Canada, the US, Australia, it doesn't matter. They were all built through extremely violent means and through genocide. My hope is that more people realise that [what Israel is doing] is part of the same imperialist structure, that one cannot exist without the other.

Since October 7, 2023, how have you been navigating voicing your support for Palestinian resistance, given the way that it has been weaponised to prevent people from speaking out against the genocide?
Honestly, I've sort of shed any fear I had. I go through the fear and I still say what I have to say. But I'm way less nervous now about what I say and how I talk than I was before October 7. Something sparked in

me and I realised that it doesn't matter what Palestinians say—whatever we say is going to be used against us, mangled, twisted—anything to make us sound like unhinged violent freaks and maniacs. That's the goal; so it doesn't matter if I say I condemn Hamas, it doesn't matter if I say I support Hamas fully, somebody somewhere is going to misconstrue that and come after me because of how I look and where I'm from. So I don't give a fuck. I don't.

Right now I will say what I have to say and, you know what, history will prove me right. And I'll know I never buckled and I never folded for the oppressor because I was 'scared'—there are way worse things in the world than being scared, believe me, I'm a Palestinian from Gaza. Do you know how easily it could have been me? Not in an interview right now but trying to figure out how the fuck I'm going to survive. It could have easily been me. Because my father was the oldest and he had to move away—that made it so I didn't have to experience that. That's why when I see my cousins and my aunts and uncles suffering, it's my suffering, it is me. I can't separate it.

There's a long history of solidarity between Black liberation struggles and Palestinian liberation struggles. How have you seen this in the past year?

I'm lucky enough that I live outside of the internet. I've seen some really good solidarity between the Black diaspora and Palestinian diaspora all over the world. I try to go back to what I experienced in real life versus the narrative that's pushed online of 'Oh, Black Americans don't care about the Palestinian struggle', or 'Palestinians are anti-Black and don't care about their struggle'.

Just last February I was invited to the Black Feminist Forum in Barbados where there were over 350 Black siblings from all over the world and we were all talking about how to mobilise, how to organise, how to show solidarity to Sudan, to Congo, to Palestine. I felt nothing but allyship, true support and true organisation focused on what we can do. At their previous forum there were no Palestinians, but this time Palestine was a big part of the entire event, and they had an actual Palestinian there. For me I'm seeing the links and the struggles connecting in real time. A lot of those people had never met a Palestinian before and then they meet me and I look like them and it's not what they see on TV. So immediately there's this conscious or subconscious breaking of what they've been told—it's like 'Oh wait, y'all can look like us? Wait a minute'. And then it's not just looking like you, but you connect on the struggle—we have similar struggles and the same oppressors.

I've seen so many lights go on in people's heads—especially when I went to Barbados. That was a really reaffirming time for me because I got to speak to so many Black women who were so touched, so interested and kept up with me and chat still to this day. They talk to me on WhatsApp and they're like, 'Hey I've been thinking about you, what's going on? I've been praying for your family.' I spoke to them when the hurricane [Beryl] hit Barbados, I was checking up on them, I was sharing their GoFundMe pages. What's better than that? We're creating links. So now maybe when somebody is talking about Palestine, they will have something to say.

That forum was made by and for Black women. The way that we organise is really something. It needs to be studied and applied to all different facets because I was mind blown. I wish every Black woman could have that experience, especially if they're a minority in their own community, like I am in Palestine. I keep going back to that moment, those five days I had over there whenever I see nonsense online about how there's no Black-Palestinian solidarity, or BS like that. No, there is—there really is and nothing you say online will deter that.

How do you see the portrayal of Afro-Palestinians within the international solidarity movement?

I didn't see any representation growing up. For a long time I thought we were the only Black Palestinian family. That's how ignorant I was. I thought anybody with my skin tone or darker than me was related to me. It was only as I grew up and I started thinking about it I thought, 'Oh, my aunt is married to a Black man—he's not related, how does that work?' [Laughs.]

After that I started looking and a few years ago there was a Black Palestinian actress and singer, Maryam Abu Khaled, and she had a video that went viral about colourism and anti-Blackness in Palestine. When I saw her video she reminded me so much of my cousin, the way she was talking, her mannerisms and I was like, 'Woah, this is great'. I'd never seen an Afro-Palestinian go viral like this with people agreeing and being so into what she was saying. She inspired me to speak out even more. Before I was super awkward—like shy. I let the fear get to me, I let the fear quiet me and silence me, especially studying journalism and seeing how that was. But seeing her made me want to speak out a bit more. And remembering my father telling me to speak out more, made me speak out more.

Just seeing a few things here and there made me think there's a community here, it's just been pushed to the side. It's one of the reasons why I started calling myself Afro-Palestinian, Black Palestinian, because I noticed that if you don't, then that part tends to get erased, whether maliciously or not. This is a part of my heritage and it needs to be said because I don't want to say 'I'm Palestinian', and then have people be like, 'Well how come you look like that?' Instead of 'Oh okay, sure you're Palestinian.' I do call myself just Palestinian sometimes, but if somebody takes out the Afro part without my consent or knowledge, I see it as erasure. And as they're [Israel and its allies] literally trying to erase us as Palestinians, I'm not going to allow that, at least for my identity, I have control over that.

In the last year I've been following two Palestinian journalists. There's Lama Jamous, the little Black girl—when I saw her I was like 'oh my god', my heart melted because I was her. When I was a kid, I wanted to be a journalist. I was the one interviewing my sister, and my mum and dad. I saw myself in her. There is another Black journalist and photographer, Hatem Hany—he is also an Afro-Palestinian. These two I've been following a lot in the past year and they've been inspirations to me. I'm really glad that their platforms have a high following and people are seeing them. For a while I thought it was just me and my family but now I can see we are a really big community, and we are Palestinian, and we also are of African descent. And I love us and I love the fact that more of us are in the public eye.

What are some of the challenges Afro-Palestinians experience in Gaza, or in Palestine more broadly?

Honestly I feel like if you had asked this question a couple of years ago my answer would have been more nuanced, but now Afro-Palestinians are facing genocide just like any other Palestinian. Believe me, Israelis do not discriminate between who they murder, they don't care if we're Black or white, pale or dark skinned. They will shoot at you. If you're Palestinian they will shoot you.

We can sit here and wax poetic about anti-Blackness but I don't think that's the conversation that needs to be had at this very moment in our history. That's not to say that Afro-Palestinians don't have their struggles—it's something that I've written about in years prior, before our annihilation wasn't so expedited. Right now I'm not going to sit down and interview my cousin and ask her how she feels about anti-Blackness. She would be like 'What the hell are you talking about, I'm trying to find water right now'. Now it's like 'Let's survive and we'll talk about it'. In the last year I haven't seen non-Black Palestinians discriminate against Black Palestinians because of their skin colour while they are trying to flee. Obviously I don't live there so I don't know, but my family has not mentioned anything of that nature, so I don't think it's at the top of the list of things they are focusing on.

There's not many Afro-Palestinians with a public profile in the diaspora. How do you manage the responses you get when you speak out about Palestine?

I do get negative responses sometimes, from different camps. It always boils down to trying to dismiss or erase my identity or part of my identity so that I fit their narrow view of the world. So whether it's a Black American person who's like 'Why do you have to mention Palestine all the time; you're Black?' Or a Palestinian person saying 'Why are you mentioning Blackness, you're Palestinian?', or a Zionist saying 'Well you're Black, you can't be Palestinian'. It's always the same thing. If I was younger I may have bought into the bullshit but in my old age now, at my big age, I know who I am and I know where I come from and I'm learning more and more. So anything you say to me … honestly you can write it in your diary, I really don't care.

I'm not over here talking to Zionists, I'm not over here trying to talk to my oppressors; I'm trying to talk to people who understand the struggle and who understand that people can be more than one thing at once. I'm not half Black, I'm fully Afro-Palestinian—I don't believe in this half nonsense. It's almost a badge of honour that I'm this thing that these Zionists can't comprehend and I go in the face of what they think a Palestinian is.

They try and throw a million and one things at me but I know who I am. I think that came with age and that came with time. When I was younger, there was a period where I didn't mention I was Palestinian because of the response I would get so I would just say I was born in Dubai and shift the conversation. But then I realised that I was literally doing the Zionists' work for them, I was erasing myself and my identity. Why, because it was complicated? Whatever reasons I had were valid then but I knew I had to move away from that and once I started learning about where I come after my father passed, that's when it really cemented. So now when I get those types of responses, I'm like, 'Well, it sounds like you don't know your history, but I know mine'.

In meeting more and more people who look like me, and just Palestinians in general, over the last few years, I have been really lucky to form amazing friendships and relationships with fellow Palestinian poets and peers. It's been a lifeline for me because they get it, I don't have to contextualise every single thing. And I've also made amazing relationships with Black women and I don't have to contextualise, it's easy, I can talk about shit and they'll get it so I focus on that. I feel like I know the Zionist playbook by now like the back of my hand. At one point you either take the bait or you don't.

What is the strength of creative writing when it comes to communicating the Palestinian struggle?

Creative writing for me has always been a way to imagine and reimagine my family's history. Especially before I had the knowledge that I do now. Looking back, I used to write a lot about family but it was always very speculative. It still is today. I think Palestinian writers in general write very speculatively; we love to imagine and reimagine our history away from the lens of the colonisers.

I think that's where creative writing comes in. I come from a journalism background, I've worked in a news office, I was an editor and that was the most painful time of my life as a Palestinian because I saw the type of news that filtered through, and the lens and the angle it had. It was just so demoralising. It was only when I moved away from that and moved towards creative writing and poetry that I started to really see the truth. That's when I started to discover the power of writing about myself and my family and our history—it's been the opposite of what I expected. I thought I would go into journalism to dig out the truth, but no, you're just going in there to become a cog in the PR machine and that was a really hard lesson for me. When

I started writing creatively, that's when people started to gravitate towards my work. When I wrote an essay about my family in Palestine, just different snippets in the past two decades about my family, my experience and all, I had so many Palestinians come up to me and say 'I could have written this, this is my experience'. So for me, creative writing has surprisingly been a way for me to find my truth and I continue to do so.

Right now the project that I'm working on gathers all of these things that I feel are so important, like how much I wanted to transcribe and write down our history when my aunt was telling it to me, meshing that with the poetry that I'm writing, meshing that with me wanting so desperately for Palestinians to come together in a time when we are being forcibly separated. All of these things are now culminating into my poetry project, One Line for Palestine. It's a crowdsourced poetry project that I created a few months ago where I asked Palestinians from all over the world to send me just one single line, and my goal was to create little poems out of them. Now after hundreds of lines, I've been working on the project and it's been the most nourishing thing in my life—it's been incredible. I'm literally putting us together on the page in a way that nobody can ever tear us apart. It's been really incredible and for the poems that I'm coming up with, you would never think there are like fifteen Palestinian writers in one poem; it just flows so organically.

This has been the type of project that I'm really into. How do I elevate us, how do I preserve us? How do I archive us? How do I reimagine the idea of the archive which has historically been so colonial, so racist, and problematic? I do that by taking back this idea of the archive and preserving our voice and our actual written word. This is the actual written word of Palestinians, not what some white guy who saw us a hundred years ago wrote. I've had submissions from the age of seven to eighty-seven. So that's what gives me hope and that's what keeps me going. And the response that I get from Palestinians—saying it's amazing and they're glad I'm doing this—it inspires them and so it inspires me.

Is there anything else you want to add?

Long live the struggle, long live the resistance, and I will always be on the side of the oppressed who are seeking liberation from their oppressor. Point blank, period. If the last year has taught me anything, it's that my words are really all I have, and I want to do everything in my power for my words to reach as many people as possible before I clock out. That's all I can do. So *vive la résistance*.

Diana Khwaelid

Diana is from Tulkarem in the northern West Bank. She has been working as a photojournalist for eight years covering the Israeli occupation, particularly in Tulkarem's refugee camps. Since October 2023, the Israeli military has invaded the city killing dozens of residents and forcibly displacing thousands of Palestinians from refugee camps. We interviewed Diana in October 2024, via an online call.

What is the situation in Tulkarem like right now?
Just now the Palestinian Ministry of Health said that there were two Palestinians killed last night, and—not only that—the Israeli soldiers mutilated the bodies. [The martyrs] were in their car, and the drone targeted them. This is normal. We consider it normal, considering what is happening in Tulkarem right now.

Were you there in the camp? Did you go to report it?
Yeah, I was there this morning, because the Israeli soldiers got into one of the areas in Nur-al-Shams refugee camp, especially in al-Nasser area, and they damaged a lot of buildings.

Did you grow up in Tulkarem? What was life like for you growing up?
Well, to be honest, the situation in Tulkarem before a year ago wasn't so bad, and also it wasn't so good. But after October 7, 2023, the situation in Tulkarem became worse, more and more. For example, if I want to give you a number of the Palestinians who have been killed since then in Tulkarem, it's 175. The Israeli government since October

2023, and actually since a year before that, started to focus its attacks more on the West Bank, and Tulkarem city has been one of the cities most targeted.

And you've been reporting on some of this, right? How is that? What is your experience as a reporter?
I have worked as a photojournalist in the field for eight years so I have seen a lot. And to be honest, it has been really hard for me to document what's going on in my city. My city used to be calm, kind of, but the political situation got much worse in the last one to two years. In my work, I lost a lot of people that I know, fellow journalists. This is one of the most difficult parts of my job, because I wasn't ready to lose people like this. I lost different people from different places. People I used to meet every single time I'd go to the camps. They saw me and said hi. They helped me, you know? I saw them from time to time, but I knew these people, they helped me a lot. And they were so kind to me. I wasn't really ready for the moment when I lost them.

What are some of the challenges of working under such a difficult environment?
The biggest challenge I have is facing the Israeli soldiers. This is the biggest problem the Palestinian communities face too. Because for the Israeli army, for example, there is no difference who you are, as long as you are a Palestinian. So the Palestinian journalists—I'm talking about myself and also my colleagues—face a lot in the field. For example, one time I got injured by a rubber bullet while I was at work. I was documenting one of the weekly demonstrations. Also I have faced tear gas at these demonstrations. My health is not really good, I can't breathe like normal people. So the gas is really bad for me.

The Israeli army, when they see a group of Palestinian journalists, they stop us. They ask for our IDs, say, 'Why are you here?', and ask lots of questions. I remember one time, in one of the villages close to Tulkarem, the soldiers took over a school, and I decided to document the situation. Five or six soldiers stopped me and they asked for my ID. One of them tried to take my cameras. And then I told them, you have no right to do that; I didn't do anything wrong. They kept me for three, four hours. So trauma like that is happening regularly.

When did you first start working as a journalist? What inspired you to start?
I was always watching the news. Because I'm Palestinian, I grew up in a political community, you know? I always saw the pictures when I was watching the news. But I didn't really imagine that one day I will become a journalist and be taking the pictures myself. But then I decided to study digital media at Birzeit University [near Ramallah]. I was working and studying at the same time. Since that time I have worked as a journalist. I'm really good at what I'm doing, and I believe in it.

How has your experience been as a female journalist?
To be honest with you, it's not easy, because I'm living in a Palestinian community. So the people here, especially the men, are used to seeing and meeting male journalists. When people see me they think I'm living outside of Palestine or from Turkey. But for me, there's no difference, like there's no difference between male and female. One of my reasons for becoming a photojournalist is that I want to prove to my community that a woman can do the job, and she can work in the field, just like a man can. Because they [the men] think the female is a weak person, and she cannot do these kinds of things. But I believe she can do it. Maybe she can do it better than a man.

Are people in the community surprised when they find out that you are from Tulkarem?
Well, a lot of people have got to know me now. But, in general, people do not expect to see a female journalist in Tulkarem. I know some guys from the camps, their daughters studied journalism in university, and they say: 'No way will I let my daughter go out in the field as a journalist, she is my only daughter, and I'm afraid for her because she's a female.' I tell them 'No, you have to let her, because she has a dream.' But you can find that sort of people here in this community.

How do you manage to keep going? What drives you to keep doing your work?
What keeps me going is that I believe the truth should be told, and also I believe the land, one day, will return to its owners. Also I like what I'm doing, I feel like I am giving a service to my community. I'm a voice like theirs, a voice for the people who have no voice.

How do you feel about the media coverage that you see of Palestine?
Well, you can find some international news agencies talking quite clearly about what's going on here. But also you can find some news agencies, or channels, that stand to the Israeli side more than the Palestinians, like CNN for example. I have seen a lot of reports by a reporter from CNN. She used to report from Gaza, and then she's moved to the Israeli side. I can see the difference from the way she speaks. When she wasn't on the Israeli side, she was talking in a powerful and human way. But I can see, because I'm a journalist, that now she stands on the Israeli side more than the Palestinian.

I'm not saying that just because I'm Palestinian. I think that as a journalist, you have to be clear, like you don't have to just take one side. You have to take two, three sides. This is your job as a journalist, to focus on the truth. It's not your job to work for just one side. That's what I believe.

You trained as a volunteer medic so that you could respond to emergencies. Could you tell us more about why you did this?
There is a group in Tulkarem that met and did the training for being medics in the camp. I took this training because I need it for my work. I mean in the field, nobody knows what you can face, right? And also to use it in my personal life, in my home, in the streets, if I saw some Palestinians who need care.

Do you have any thoughts about the roles of Palestinian women within the wider international solidarity movement?
Actually, you can find a lot of Palestinian women activists, but the level has become lower than before. For example, in the Second Intifada [2002–5], women were in the first line before the men. But now, from my experience, if I find a woman activist in the field that will be a great thing. Because usually I don't see women. It depends on the situation. Inside the city there are no soldiers, and you can find a lot of women in activities there. But, for example, if we are documenting a difficult situation, then it's hard to find an active Palestinian woman.

How has Palestinian society changed since the Second Intifada, to mean that women are not in these roles?

Recently, I was documenting the situation in Tulkarem refugee camp. The old people here, particularly in the camps, are the ones who have lived through the First and Second Intifadas. One man said to me that the recent attack [Israeli military invasion and siege of Tulkarem] was the worst since the 1970s, and another said it was the worst since the Second Intifada. These old people, they really know the difference. So I think that the situation in Palestine has become much worse.

I often don't find women activists at demonstrations these days, or other places like that. I think the Palestinians, both the men and women, are becoming more afraid. Even the men themselves, they have to think twice before going into the field. So it's even harder for women.

How would you describe your politics, your beliefs, the things you would like to change about the world?

I prefer to present myself as a Palestinian, that's it. The Palestinians have different parties and groups, resistance groups for example. But I believe that, for the Israel government, there's no difference as long as you are a Palestinian. It doesn't matter which side you are from.

I remember I met a guy from the camp, and I asked him 'Why do you continue [fighting]?' On that day the Israeli soldiers had killed most of the Palestinian fighters inside the camp. But still, you can see the Palestinian fighters continue to carry weapons. So I was just curious. He said to me, 'As long as there is occupation, there is going to be resistance.'

And that's right, that's why the resistance exists. The reason is because the occupation exists, right? If there's no occupation, there's no fighters. The Palestinians dream of living a normal life. And like any people in this world, they have a right. The Palestinians in this community have been living under occupation for more than seventy-four years. It's time to let these people live in freedom. If you get down to the streets, the people talk about politics all the time. Even myself, when I go to bed at night. I always check the news. So all my life, even my personal life, focuses on politics.

If you want to talk about Palestinians in this community, we're not talking about people who have no relationship with politics. Most of them, they have no personal life. They just focus on the political side. And this is crazy. Even myself, I became crazy. I have no personal life. I can't live as a normal person.

The occupation, they took our dreams, they take our freedom. They took everything, even our soul. I'm talking right now because I'm alive, but also I'm not really alive. Nobody knows what's inside me. Journalism has changed me a lot. I have seen a lot of Palestinians killed in front of me. At night, I cannot sleep very well. My food regime has changed, I cannot eat like normal people. I lost weight. Everything which is going on here in the West Bank affects our lives a lot. In the street, I find that you cannot laugh.

Has this become the norm, that people don't want to express joy because of everything that's happening right now?
When we see what has happened in Gaza since October 7 [2023], for us in the West Bank these are our people. Same blood, right? Even if they live in a different area of Palestine, they are still our people. So the Palestinians, they have changed. Even myself, because of what we have seen in the news about all that's going on in Gaza. So many children. I would like to say that it's a genocide, not a war.

For myself, if I want to have fun in my personal life, I have to think twice. I smoke shisha, but if I want to go out and smoke, I have to think 'Should I do that?'

What are your hopes for what might happen now, in terms of the situation in Palestine?
As I told you before, the situation has become much worse. Nobody knows what's going to happen tomorrow. Probably the Israeli government has huge plans for the future. And even the Palestinians living here in the West Bank, they started to say that we cannot live in this situation anymore. We are not feeling safe. We are suffering a lot, so it's time to start a new life. Can you imagine, in the next two years, how many Palestinians will stay in Palestine? The Israeli government plans to push the Palestinians out of Palestine, and they are pushing us beyond our limits. Even in the refugee camps, thousands of Palestinians have left because they lost their homes.

Where do they go?
To their neighbours. Or, if possible they find another apartment outside of the camp, just for a while, because they have children, they have a family.

However much I try, I cannot really describe all that's going on here. I feel a lot of pressure inside me for these words to get out. But still I can't fully describe the situation.

There was a recent F-16 attack on a café in Tulkarem refugee camp, and Israeli politicians have been saying that they should treat the West Bank like Gaza. It seems like the cities in the north—Jenin, Tulkarem, Tubas—are bearing the brunt of the violence?

The last act of genocide you mentioned at the café, that was last Thursday evening [October 3, 2024]. Eighteen Palestinian people were killed that night [the number later rose to twenty]. Two children and two women among them, and thirteen of them were civilians. That never happened before in Tulkarem. Even the Palestinians from the camps said that this was the first time since the Second Intifada that the Israeli government used that kind of plane.

They think they have a right to target the Palestinians. And for them, there is no difference between Palestinian civilians or fighters. And this is the problem, because they are different. They were watching six fighters inside the camp, and they targeted them. But they don't give a fuck about the other people who are in the area. There's a building beside the cafe, which was targeted that day. There are two or three families living in this building, and the Israeli government definitely knew that. But they don't care. They really don't care. A whole family has been killed, the father, the mother, and two children.

The Palestinians in the West Bank, they know that it's getting really serious. Recently, I have been documenting an incident where four Palestinians were targeted in their car. They are from two different camps in Nablus. They were targeted by special Israeli forces in daylight in the middle of the city.

My colleagues started to say to me recently that I should stay away from fighters' groups. The news agencies are saying it too. Because nobody knows what's going to happen. For the Israeli military, there's no difference, even if there's one, or two, or three Palestinian journalists killed in an operation. There's no issue for them if there's five or ten Palestinian civilians killed for one fighter. Two of my Palestinian journalist colleagues from the West Bank are under arrest right now and are in jail. One of them is from Tulkarem and the other from

Nablus. They got arrested by Israeli forces. Why? Because they're doing their job, covering the news.

Is there anything that you would want from left-wing journalists, media organisations, or trade unions outside of Palestine? Is there a way for them to stand in solidarity with Palestinian journalists?
I think all the journalists around the world have a message. Our message is focused on the truth. We believe as journalists, both in Palestine and globally, that the truth should be told whatever happens. So my message as a Palestinian journalist to the international journalist is, please don't just take one side. If you want to write a story, you need to hear accounts from both sides. And if you hear from both sides, you can then decide.

There are over 150 Palestinian journalists who have been killed in Gaza. What is the position of international journalists about that? What is their personal opinion about that? This is genocide. So what is your position? Because if they want to stand with me, I don't want them to stand with me just because I'm Palestinian. I am speaking as a journalist. Even if we have different languages, different nationalities, we still have the same message, the same goal, right?

I would love to see the international journalists organise a demonstration or a protest for Palestinian journalists outside of Palestine. Journalists around the world have a right to move freely, to do their job without problems.

I know I have been working as a photojournalist in the field for eight years now. But I'm not going to lie to you—I'm afraid. A lot of people I know often ask me [about fear], when they see me carrying my cameras and my press jacket, they ask me this question. They are surprised because I am a woman. I tell them I am a journalist but I am still a human being, of course I'm afraid. We're talking about a conflict zone. So the area where we are working as Palestinian journalists is more dangerous than any place in this world, because, as I told you before, for Israeli soldiers or the Israeli government: there's no difference, as long as you are a Palestinian.

We want to move freely. Why should we feel afraid when we go to the field? But every single time I go to work, I don't know if I'm going to come back safely to my home. Every single time I say hi to my family, they check if I'm okay, because they know that maybe I will get shot.

Something like what happened to the Palestinian-American journalist Shireen Abu Akleh. She was reporting what was happening in Jenin, she was wearing a press jacket. And every single person in the area, including the soldiers and the sniper who shot her knew that she was press. A lot of Palestinian journalists have a family, they have children. And every time they go out, they don't know if they will get back safe.

I have some problems. I lost my attention, and this is one of my big problems as a journalist. Yesterday, when I was sitting with some of my friends who are journalists too, we were talking, and I found out that I'm not the only one with this problem. For example, we forget people's names when we meet them in the street. People say 'Hey, how are you?' They know our names, but for a few seconds, we can't remember their names.

Do you think these memory problems are because of the things that you've experienced and seen?

Yeah, absolutely, because I wasn't like this before. If you asked me about my memory six or seven years ago, it wasn't like that. I had a strong memory. But not anymore. We are starting to lose ourselves. We look normal. We speak normally, but we are not normal. And because we are journalists, we feel ashamed to share this information with other people. I'm a journalist, so I have to show the people around me that I am active, I am strong, and I am smart. But if the people around you see that you are not active anymore, or if they see that you are suffering, it's going to be a problem. People have a particular picture of us, and we need to keep up [this illusion]. That's another of our problems.

Shahd Abusalama

Shahd is from Jabalia refugee camp in northern Gaza. When this interview was carried out, Shahd was living in Sheffield, UK. She is an activist, academic, writer, and artist, and also dances dabke, the traditional folk dance of Palestine. We interviewed Shahd in December 2020, via an online call.

Why did you move to the UK?

I got a scholarship to do my master's degree at SOAS—the School of Oriental and African Studies—in London in 2014. Luckily I made it there; it was always a dream for me, ever since I was a kid, to go to the UK and study and I had made multiple attempts, even for my BA degree.

During my BA the situation in Gaza wasn't good, it was really difficult to go out. The siege was very suffocating and choking and I remember applying for scholarships and getting really close to getting my goal—my ambition—done and then the siege happened and the borders were closed in my face. I even applied for Birzeit University [in the West Bank, near Ramallah] and I couldn't even go there [because of the Israeli siege of Gaza].

Was it difficult to get a visa?

I mean, visas are difficult for people in the Global South in general, but the thing that many people don't understand is that in the case of Gaza and its unique circumstances, it's probably easier to get the visa than it is to get out of Gaza. Then there's crossing the borders. This is the reason why many people in the Gaza Strip get their ambitions crushed at the doorsteps of Rafah and Erez and many people lose their jobs outside just because they decide to come back to Gaza. They might be working outside and decide to come back for a holiday and to visit their families, and they'd end up getting stuck for months and losing their work permit and means of income.

It was 2013 when I was trying to leave, but thankfully I had two scholarships—one to Turkey and another to the UK. I managed to use the one to Turkey as a safe transit to the UK. I finally managed, after weeks and weeks of tries, to cross the border. Turkey was more tolerant in terms of students arriving late—they gave the Palestinians a sort of special condition. However, it wasn't the case with the UK so I was kind of lucky.

How did you first become involved in politics and activism?
This 'activism' is a funny term for me, because we Palestinians are born into a complex situation and 'activism'—what people call 'activism'—is almost a way of life for us.

I was born into a politically active family. My dad was an activist and he spent a total of fifteen years in Israeli jails for his membership of the Popular Front for the Liberation of Palestine (PFLP) [a revolutionary socialist political party, historically part of the Arab Nationalist Movement and later the Palestine Liberation Organization]. All of these political parties are considered terrorists under the Israeli occupation.

All my family really—men and women—were to some extent actively engaged in what was happening, but it was really a way of life, a way to overcome our feelings of helplessness. My parents were very conscious about, for example, the weekly protest in solidarity with Palestinian political prisoners that is held every Monday at the Red Cross in Gaza: we were there every Monday, never missed it. The oppression comes to your home, comes to your neighbourhood. We grew up very aware that the situation was very oppressive and unfair, and oppression breeds resistance.

Was it similar for others your age who were growing up around you?
I think it's entrenched in the psyche of the Palestinians to reject and refuse the oppression befalling them. How people express this differs from one individual to another, but ever since I was a kid I was going to cultural centres with members of my own generation, engaging in all sorts of activities, with Palestine and our lived experiences at the heart

of it. In our context, there's a very blurry line between the cultural and the political, the personal and the collective, and everything somehow intersects in our reality, ever since we were kids.

For example, you ask any child in Gaza, 'Where do you come from?' They don't tell you, 'Oh, we come from Jabalia', or 'We come from Rimal', or 'We come from Beit Lahia' (I'm naming neighbourhoods in Gaza). They say, 'We come from Beit-Jirja', or 'We come from Jaffa', or 'We come from Isdud' [places that were ethnically cleansed in 1948, and now lie within the Green Line].

Whether they acknowledge it or not, whether they're consciously aware of it or not, this answer is very political and connotes how the oppressive situation generates political awareness among people. Children grow up long before their time, against their parents' wishes for them to live a more peaceful life than theirs.

In Jabalia refugee camp, I lived through what people experienced as an 'ongoing Nakba'. In 2000, when I was nine, the Second Intifada erupted, fundamentally shaping my generation's consciousness about our surrounding realities, the land, and our place in it.

Before this Palestinian uprising, my parents had always tried to reassure us of our safety, with phrases like 'the occupation does not kill children, only adults'. On September 30, 2000, however, when the schools were on strike, I was sitting with my parents watching television, when the murder in Gaza of twelve-year-old Muhammad al-Durrah appeared on all the news bulletins. I remember my mum covering my sight in an attempt to obstruct my vision, while urging my dad to switch channels. She could not hide it for long, however, as Mohammed and the last cry of his injured father, 'Mat al-walad' (the boy has died), became icons of the new Intifada which would last the next five years.

Israeli attacks on Palestinians intensified to the extent that UNRWA [United Nations Relief and Works Agency] schools repeatedly carried out mock evacuations as practice for all children and teachers, to be prepared in case of any future attack against schools.

My parents, like others, struggled to provide answers for the questions from me and my siblings regarding the unjust reality we were born into, and the collective lived experience made us grow up sooner than they hoped. My generation grasped the basics at an early age; we are a dispossessed and stateless people struggling for liberation under Israeli occupation. This theme dominated all our mourning and celebrations.

As well as being active around the occupation and oppression of Palestinians, have you also channelled that into other issues and campaigns?

Definitely. I feel strong affinity with the Irish, Black, Kashmiri, and Kurdish struggles, for example. I think for us this kind of reaction is a matter of survival; it reminds us that we are not struggling alone. It's almost an attempt to reclaim our humanity in an immensely dehumanising situation. Many people try to channel this negative energy imposed on us from these mechanisms of oppression into positive things. We understand what oppression means. We understand what it means to be singled out because of your race, ethnicity, or religion. We understand this very well and this doesn't come from an abstract understanding; we didn't learn it from books but from lived experiences.

What are some of the differences between political organising in the UK and when you were in Gaza?

Back in Gaza, I was active on several fronts, at community cultural centres and organisations advocating for Palestinian political prisoners and in BDS. As I previously said, trying to transform this experience into something positive is truly a matter of survival and so you find Palestine, despite the odds, exporting artists—internationally renowned artists, musicians, you name it—conductors, writers, intellectuals, all professions really. I think it is also because of our understanding of the urgency and the meaning of life.

Something that I felt when I came to the UK, something that always challenged me, is our different understandings of the urgency. It's like people don't seem to understand that actions they may take could be a matter of life and death, and I've always felt that I was working at a different pace from others. This made me at times feel frustrated with people being lazy or not acting proactively enough. I was always the person trying to agitate and get a statement out or get the protest organised, or something like that, and I think it's really because other people don't understand how almost every minute in Palestine is a matter of life and death.

It never occurred to me when I crossed the Rafah border that I wasn't going to go back, never. But then the siege even prohibited us from returning to our refugee camps. I'm a refugee; I was born a refugee and then I find myself in a completely different setting and from afar watching my family, my loved ones, friends, and everybody that I care about surviving through siege, military occupation, and apartheid and subjugated to daily forms of violence. It fucks up your mind, really. You feel powerless as you follow the news and it's just constant horror. Especially in Gaza, which Israel treats as a laboratory where they could develop innovative ways of control, applying mechanisms that were never probably used in any other context in the history of humanity—it's just incredible how normalised these extreme injustices are.

When you know the kind of reality that people live there ... By the time I left, I'd survived countless wars and so I know how real the threat is. So it's like, we're not joking: when we're campaigning we're actually trying to end the material complicity and oppression, we're really trying to save more lives, more innocent lives, from falling prey to this inhumane situation.

What does rest mean for someone who is restless? What does that look like?

I struggle with the concept of self-care that is very widely used in the UK. I wonder what self-care and mental health are when oppression is continuous, you feel it under your skin.

I know that no one comes out of such inhumane situations without being affected and I'm only human to be affected by such things. But we find consolation and power in solidarity, in nurturing hope, and hope is revived from these collective actions, from being confrontational against these normalised dehumanisations. I see this as care not only for the self but for the community. Sometimes I get people saying, 'Oh, you should rest.' They say it in so many different ways of course but, I don't know, how can I detach myself from what is happening? I don't know, how can you detach yourself, how can you actually rest?

How do you see your position or role as someone living outside of Palestine? Do you get to organise with other Palestinians in the UK and what are some of the challenges of being active from the outside?

Living such an uncertain life as a Palestinian leaves you—as you said—restless and just unable to detach yourself from what is happening because even if you detach yourself, it follows you everywhere.

It's always beautiful to connect with anybody on the basis of defending Palestinian human rights, but especially Palestinians. In the UK, for the first time, I met people from all over Palestine. When I was in Palestine that was a dream that was almost impossible [it is impossible for Palestinians from Gaza to visit the other parts of Palestine]. So this segregation and dispersion we have endured added another layer of attachment to other Palestinian communities across Palestine, the Arab world, and globally. Apartheid structures seek to fragment the Palestinian social fabric and geography. So it's always really exciting when I connect to people from other cities or other towns and you realise how similar you are, and how we didn't need to explain ourselves to each other because it was sort of understood. Yes, we were probably subjected to different extremes of violence but we know that at least, suffering, exile, and the burning desire to be free unites us. These shared experiences make us connected almost immediately.

It is actually really inspirational to see Palestinians who have never been to Palestine but are very passionate about the cause, and speak Arabic almost fluently, probably in a much more perfected Palestinian accent than mine. Such encounters make me realise how the roots truly run deep. All this is just like the wonders of hope and beauty, and confirmation that the Zionist project has failed. I talk about friends like, for example, Huda Ammori [a British Palestinian who co-founded the direct-action group Palestine Action], she's never been to Palestine. So many countless examples I have in mind. They have such a connection to Palestine; it's real and inspirational. The Zionist project thought that the old would die and the young would forget. They were so wrong.

How would you describe your politics? Do you find any particular labels helpful?

I'm comfortable with the words 'feminist' and 'Palestinian'. I would say that leftist politics are very much part of my upbringing, even before I even understood what Marxism and communism was. It's probably related to my parents being involved with the PFLP. But I think there are some values and principles you just have to agree with as long as you're a decent human. It's not a matter of left or right.

With feminism, when I was younger, I didn't understand the word very well and I was like sort of … [laughs] it's funny, I was kind of resisting the word and associating it with Western things. I had this tendency to rebel against anything that is Western associated [laughs]. To this day, the pop music that we hear all the time, I see people my age singing along and they're so hyped and I'm like 'What is this song?' I still find comfort in listening to Arabic music and films after seven years in exile. You know, I can't avoid Netflix, especially in quarantine [the COVID-19 lockdowns and restrictions], but I try to watch with a critical eye.

I sort of associated feminism with a Western discourse that imposes their outlook on others without considering the specific socio-political contexts that give women's movements in the Global South their distinctive features. We heard what happened in France against women [who wanted to wear a niqab, or veil] and how Afghanistan was invaded in the name of protecting women. All these double standards were legitimated in the name of feminism. At that time I didn't have enough maturity to understand that the problem lies in how imperial powers hijacked feminist thought to gloss over their prejudices and crimes.

Now we see this enacted bluntly by an apartheid state pretending to be democratic, and even feminist, because its military service applies to both men and women. The paradox also applied to Israel's self-proclaimed identity as 'a democratic Jewish state', which suggests, as many Palestinian citizens of Israel argue, that it is only democratic to Jews. The term itself contradicts itself, especially when you understand how it's based on systems of settler colonialism and apartheid; 20 percent of Israel's citizens are Palestinians and they don't have the same rights as Jews and the rest of Palestinians [who aren't citizens of Israel] are either exiled or crammed into Bantustan-like enclaves.[1] This reality exposes the absurdity of [Zionists and Israeli politicians] who speak on behalf of justice and human rights, concepts which are only

1 Bantustans were the isolated Black enclaves set up by the apartheid-era government of South Africa. The isolation of Palestinian communities from each other by Israel is often compared to the Bantustans.

monopolised to certain groups and certain races. Similarly, feminism has been hijacked; the human rights discourse has been hijacked.

Everything that we thought was beautiful and represented a sense of humanity is hijacked by powers that are trying to find legitimation for their actions through empty terms that are used but not enacted. I think that this is the same problem that ran with revolutionary thoughts and ideas that our human civilisation brought to existence such as Marxism, communism, and socialism; they're beautiful and yes, there might be limitations here and there but in essence they're revolutionary in the way they empowered the oppressed and advocated an alternative reality to that imposed by the exploitative capitalist class. But the way it's practised, the way that people in power hijack those ideas, is the alarming thing.

Do you see your creative practice and dance as being linked with politics?

I've already said it's hard to separate things; the line between the political and the cultural, the collective and the personal is very blurry in the context of Palestine. I'm really thankful that my family encouraged our engagement with these artistic means of expression since childhood. I didn't understand how much they helped me to survive, but they truly did. I was dancing dabke probably before I started walking—this is a running joke in the family. My siblings, cousins, and I joined local troops in celebration of our culture, following my mum who was a member of a Jerusalem-based troop in the 1980s.

Dabke represents an expression of identity, of resistance, and of pride in our cultural heritage. It has multiple meanings: its practice is also about celebrating life, joy, community, and togetherness. I also found power in drawing and singing. Most of my drawings were in black and white, partially because I didn't have access to art resources. I remember one time while I was in Gaza, an activist who knew from online that I liked drawing, brought me gifts from outside—paper, that paper that makes drawing a lot easier and more defined, special paper for drawing; we didn't have that. I was really happy. Reflecting back I realise that I sought these means of expression and healing long before I even realised how therapeutic and powerful they are as means of intervention and communication. They definitely offered an escape from that feeling of helplessness we often felt under Israeli oppression.

I'm looking from a distance now, and I realise how so many elements in our Palestinian culture are basically founded on community and communal solidarity—you see this in a lot of things. You see this, for example, in the folk dance of Palestine—in dabke, and how people enact it. In funerals and festivals of freedom and things like that. And peoples' compassion with each other—I would say that capitalism still failed to make people centred on themselves in Palestine because of this collective experience and this sense of community as well. I think it's life-changing and cultivates hope and resilience. But I also know how important solidarity is in these sorts of settings and how it can be really a front of resistance against such mechanisms of oppression.

When I came to the UK so many elements of my life were missing, and I was constantly nostalgic and missing this sort of dynamic life that I used to have back home. I also really believe in how meaningful dabke is and how expressive it is of the Palestinian resistance and cultural heritage. The narrative of resistance is embodied in the songs, the way our bodies move and the way people come together, holding hands and dancing together, there's a lot of beauty to it. As soon as I arrived in London, one of my first questions was 'Is there a dabke group here?' Luckily there was a group called Zaytouna (as in olive). They had been dancing for over ten years and were on the verge of collapsing due to internal tensions, so I joined them for barely a year before the group sort of dissolved.

I was still determined not to miss this element in my life. So I joined with a few women who still wanted to carry on dancing, and we formed our own women's group. We called it Hawiyya (Arabic for 'ID') and we established it in 2017. We were only four women and now we're eight, so we're growing slowly but steadily and we choreograph our own performances and have travelled throughout the UK performing dabke. We've done refreshing collaborations with Palestinian dabke groups back home such as Lajee (Bethlehem), El-Funoun (Ramallah), and Layali Al-Farah (Gaza).

The power of dabke makes people with minimal to no knowledge about Palestine fall in love with the cause and become so curious about learning; you know it sort of instigates this curiosity from people. I think that it's really important to remind others that the Palestinian people are holding onto their heritage and have vibrant things to be celebrated, aside from the widespread images that associate Palestinian lives with violence.

How are you feeling now about the situation for Palestinian people and the way things are in the world at the moment? Where do you see the hope?

Sometimes I get super depressed. There are so many worrying signs, such as the rise of the right wing and xenophobia. I think that's also why cultivating hope is a matter of survival. My personal experience outside Palestine raised my awareness of the surrounding net of oppressive politics and practices.

After I finished my master's degree, I ended up living through the inhumane process of asylum seeking, as the doors to Gaza were still closed. That was really re-traumatising but also eye-opening to British society, and European society in general. I was campaigning for refugee rights with Women for Refugee Women, Movement for Justice by Any Means Necessary, and SOAS Goes to Calais. We grew connected with other groups campaigning for refugee rights across Europe and in Turkey. With my background of originally being born a refugee, I became very invested in this issue, hoping to save future generations from this vicious circle of violence.

The scale of double standards and hypocrisy is just incredible, and we see this in Europe where the motto 'never again' originated. The targeting of other minority groups—the Muslims and Arabs and everyone who's considered 'other'—amid the rise of the right-wing policies that scapegoat these communities is really alarming and makes you wonder if any lessons have been learned.

The system is deeply complicit in perpetuating violence against the Palestinians and enabling Israeli apartheid and the crimes against us to the extent that we feel we can never really break free of violence. Whether in Palestine or outside, all of these intersecting mechanisms of violence are chasing me wherever I go; I see them in the brands normalised on supermarket shelves, brands such as Puma [which sponsored the Israeli Football Association until 2024], banks such as HSBC [which invests in companies that arm Israel], not to mention the media discourse that shamelessly reproduces the Israeli narrative.

That's why I actively sought campaigning groups; for me those constituted windows of hope and potential change that feels more achievable when our energies unite. So yeah, there are signs of hope but I think people really need to step up to those challenges, because we are facing times like no other before. I think the pandemic uncovered some of these structural inequalities globally, and hopefully it made people more aware of how interconnected we are, or maybe I'm just feeling optimistic. I hope I'm not alone in thinking this.

I think what is happening in the Labour Party is alarming—the deliberate conflation between anti-Zionism and antisemitism and between Zionism and Judaism is really troubling, has a very chilling effect, and shows how powerful the Zionist lobby is. Even anti-Zionist Jews are not exempt from these silencing attempts. Jeremy Corbyn [former leader of the Labour Party in Britain] once gave the impression that another form of politics that is biased to the oppressed and the poor is possible, but the organised Zionist witch hunt and his replacement with a self-proclaimed Zionist tell us that there's still a long way to go.

In one's bubble of safety and comfort, it is easy to assume that we enjoy freedom and equality, but all these are a facade, and they don't really reflect the genuine reality of things. If only people understand how they are part of enabling this system, and how their privileges could deprivilege others. Taxpayers cannot be considered passive once we understand how their tax money is being invested in funds that go into the arms trade or into facilitating those mechanisms of oppression. It's the same with citizens who have the right to vote but help bring someone like Trump into power and uphold anti-refugee attitudes, or pro-Israel, or pro-apartheid values. The vote has a weight and if you're a responsible citizen, you shouldn't be thinking in terms of individualistic interests.

In this time and age, I think it's a must that we live with open and critical eyes, because otherwise we're eaten within. First it was the Gypsies, then the disabled, then the homosexuals, and then the Jews and Black people, then the Armenians and the Bosnians, and the Palestinians and the Muslims ... the scapegoat will only be changing if we don't really open our eyes to stand firm for our human values and for freedom, social justice, and equality for all.

I do believe in the power of people and I do believe that hopefully Palestine will have its South Africa moment. The BDS campaign is very, very powerful; it's growing. The fact that Israel is delegating a whole ministry to combat the BDS—The Strategic Affairs Ministry [an Israeli government ministry established to counter the success of the BDS movement], this signifies how threatened and insecure they are. The use of hard power by Israel and other states further reveals the real threats that such peaceful movements are posing. Before, the use of soft power may have made it difficult to see, but now the police and the intelligence agencies are using hard power.[2] Activists are being jailed, protesters are being attacked with tear gas canisters and even shot in the streets in places that claim to be democratic and to value human rights. We also see refugees, including Palestinians, dying at the shorelines and borders of the EU due to xenophobic policies. The use of hard power is an indication that hegemonic systems are weakened, and it's also opening people's eyes to what's really happening. If you're safe today, you might not be tomorrow.

---

2 Hard power commonly means the use of forceful power such as physical repression, invasions, arrest, and imprisonment. It can also refer to the wielding of economic power such as sanctions. Soft power relates to a more subtle form of power where a state tries to put forward arguments that serve its objectives. Israel's political use of false accusations of antisemitism against BDS organisers is an example of this.

Shahd Abusalama (2024 Update)

Shahd is from Jabalia refugee camp in northern Gaza, and is currently living in Barcelona. We interviewed Shahd for the second time on November 5, 2024, via an online video call. We asked her for her thoughts on the situation for her family and for other Palestinians four years on, in the midst of the Gaza genocide.

Do you feel that things have changed since we interviewed you last?
Reading through my interview from 2020, I realise that no, nothing has changed, apart from the level of barbarity we are fighting against. Back then we believed that the oppression was not sustainable—the suffocating siege, the air strikes, the frequent acts of 'mowing the lawn', the apartheid policies, the massacres, we thought it couldn't go on.

However, because of the impunity and the unaccountability, this settler-colonialist, capitalist project has been enabled to commit a genocide in full view of the whole world, while also terrorising Lebanon and Syria and expanding domination over their lands. Here we are, we are living through a genocide, the annihilation of our people, ethnic cleansing, and no one can do anything.

The West is complicit, many countries have an active role and are supporting the capitalist project. For them, exemplified in the voice of Jared Kushner, Gaza is nothing but 'a waterfront property' with rich resources which would bring 'valuable' gains for Israel. Meanwhile, Daniella Weiss has been described by CNN, the BCC, and other Western mainstream media as 'the godmother of the Israeli settler movement'. She claimed at a recent Likud- [Israel's governing political party] backed conference that thousands of settlers from other countries have signed up to her vision and are ready to move to Gaza and make it 'Jewish'.

These people are working towards realising settler-colonial capitalist fantasies, ignoring the fact that Gaza is home to 2.3 million Palestinians, most of whom are descendants of already stolen Palestinian lands in 1948, and are now facing mass extermination and starvation. They are openly gaining profit at the expense of our lives, the genocide of our people and of our material world, our culture. This is our 'Gaza Nakba' being rolled out, as described by Israeli minister Avi Dichter back in November 2023, but we are still meant to be Israel's well-behaved victims.

There is an international network of politicians and arms and fossil fuel traders that are enabling Israel to maintain its military occupation, apartheid regime, and 'to finish off the job' in Gaza. The Gaza genocide is the outcome of a long-standing dehumanising discourse that legitimated this rogue state [Israel], and normalised diplomatic, military, academic, and economic relations with it.

People like me don't have the luxury of thinking about the 'day after', but I would hate to live in a world that condones genocidal Israel. As a person grieving dozens of loved cousins, probably hundreds of neighbours, friends, and teachers, while continuing to worry about the fate of others surviving under blockaded, destroyed, and constantly bombed Gaza, dismantling Zionism is a minimum requirement. This would be the minimum compensation for all the pain and terror they have inflicted upon us for generations.

Beit Hanoun, Beit Lahia, and Jabalia, where I was born and raised, have been facing relentless and indiscriminate bombing, targeting concentrations of displaced Palestinian survivors wherever they are. This ongoing brutal siege is part of the 'General's Plan' [proposed by Israeli General Giora Eiland], where politicians have openly fantasised plans of mass extermination and ethnic cleansing.

We learnt a few days ago that our family building in Al-Saftawi Street near Jabalia refugee camp was razed to the ground, after it had survived Israeli soldiers bombing it and setting it on fire in previous invasions of northern Gaza.

My home was targeted three times since the genocide started—first it was bombed, then it was burned, and now it has been razed to the ground. Despite its unliveable conditions, it remained standing, offering shelter to destitute families of relatives and neighbours whose homes were flattened. But now even this is no longer possible.

Our house is just like 95 percent of homes in Gaza now. Gone. They want Gaza empty. According to the Israeli foreign minister, there are no civilians left in the north part of Gaza now, and they have proceeded with their mass extermination policies accordingly. They have divided up northern Gaza in three parts.

A neighbour next door, whose home was also reduced to rubble, reported the news at a horrific cost. Al-Saftawi Street, which links the Governorate of Northern Gaza to Gaza City, had been inaccessible. There were frequent explosions, accompanied by news of Israel flattening our neighbourhood and targeting every moving being.

During an apparent period of calm, my neighbour went to check on our homes. On his way back, soon after confirming our fears, an Israeli quadcopter shot him in his head and back, leaving him on a hospital bed between life and death [quadcopters are small remote-controlled drones that Israeli forces are using to kill and maim people].

An Israeli quadcopter also murdered my maternal cousin Jaber Ali on December 10, 2024, during a similar endeavour to check on his home in Beit-Lahia, which Israel bombed. In March 2024, Jaber had become a father to a baby boy, Kamal. Displacement, mass bombing, and starvation renders Kamal's survival uncertain.

Jaber was a young family man who dreamt of a future, now erased by Israel. His young widow and son are now sheltering with other family survivors in a partially demolished home in west Gaza. The dangers forced neighbours to bury Jaber where they found his body, denying his family a chance to say goodbye or give him a dignified burial.

We are now more scared than ever of enduring the same fate of our grandparents, who were dispossessed and displaced in 1948 and never allowed to return, thanks to Israel's racist legal and military policies. But no one can take the right to return to our lands and rebuild our homes, no matter what.

Where are you living now and how are you and your parents?

My parents and brother Mohammed and his wife and two daughters—the second born a month before the start of the genocide—managed to flee Gaza. I couldn't stay in the UK, so we're living in an apartment in Barcelona. We're lucky because one of my sisters has a Spanish visa, but how can we eat or do anything normal when our people are being annihilated? With six members of my family now around me, I feel even more immersed with all our aunts and uncles, cousins, neighbours, and friends and stuck in the time of genocide.

When my family had to flee northern Gaza, they saw dead body parts on the way, among other horrors. They were guided by a quadcopter. We have lost dozens of people in my extended family, including twenty-three in a bombing in Jabalia on October 23, 2023, an event I documented for an article published on *Declassified UK*. My cousin Khalil became single in one day during this massacre. One day he had a wife and children, the next day he was a single person. Ever since, bad news has been raining non-stop as a result of escalating, indiscriminate bombardment that keeps pushing my family survivors to endless displacements.

Meanwhile, in Spain, which many people think is more pro-Palestine than many European countries, the government is still selling arms to Israel. They've sold over a million euros of weapons since October 2023, while Israel is engaged in 'plausible genocide'.

When I can't bear being in the flat any longer and watching the videos of my people being exterminated, I go outside with my Palestine flag. Not on a march though. Marches are on weekends, when those who are privileged can join them, as if genocide doesn't happen on weekdays. Genocide doesn't come and go, we must understand that we are living in a time of genocide.

Most people are good, and many smile or acknowledge me with my flag. But one time, I carried it to a kite-flying event we organised to welcome my brother and his family; they arrived in Barcelona around mid-September. A man told me to take it down, a woman and a child were with him. I replied saying that 'the children being slaughtered in Gaza are younger than your daughter.' He said, 'What about the children being killed in Israel too?' I said that over twenty thousand children have been killed in Palestine with thousands missing under the rubble. He said, 'What about all the children killed on October 7?' I said that thousands of infants have been born and killed during the genocide. Then I started shouting 'Free, free Palestine'. I was waving the flag over his head—not the stick, just the flag—I waved it and he got very angry. He started manhandling me, pushing other men that had tried to intervene and keep him away.

What actions do you think people supporting Palestine, especially in the countries heavily involved in the genocide, should be doing differently?

The ongoing genocide in Gaza has galvanised a persistent, creative, and disruptive global uprising for Palestine, including workers and activists shutting down arms factories and disrupting trade, and youth-led university encampments and national protests. I hope that such brave actions keep coming, not seasonally, but with unwavering commitment and determination, because the violence is structural and continuous. Never forget that this is not the Palestinians' fight alone, and the bigger the privilege, the larger the duty.

Together with this dynamic global uprising for Palestine, the repression of voices exposing Israeli brutality and demanding accountability is escalating, with protesters and activists risking vilification and dismissal from employment, police brutality, and arbitrary detention. Silencing those resisting with the Palestinians is a partnership in Israel's crimes of apartheid and genocide and needs to be resisted collectively.

Palestinians in the West are particularly vulnerable as we continue to be subjected to endless campaigns of defamation and censorship, criminalised and hounded for existing, sharing our experiences, and expressing our aspirations for freedom, justice, equality, and return. The level of policing that Palestinian survivors are subjected to, even as we experience genocide and ethnic cleansing one generation after the other, is scandalous and further exposes Israel's desperation to silence the truth and escape accountability.

My brother Majed Abusalama faces court in Germany after social media companies violated his information and digital rights, making him vulnerable to the oppressive German authorities. They are now trying to incriminate him for posts such as 'from the river to the sea, Palestine will be free'.

Our allies should not shy away from supporting our liberation struggle against this super military imperial power by any means necessary. Israel has no so-called right to exist as an apartheid state of the systematic ethnic cleansing of Palestinians and has no so-called right to self-defence against the people they have repeatedly massacred, dispossessed, starved, and occupied. Israel has made a mockery of Judaism and all religions and conventions and needs to be treated as the pariah state it is.

The land is ours and victory will be ours too. Israel needs to face the fact that its end is coming as they can't expect to get away with committing a genocide with no consequences. Keep on speaking truth to power, exposing and disrupting the malicious activities of those complicit in enabling Israeli crimes, and ensuring that international law is respected. Don't accept the normalisation of Israeli embassies in your countries and make sure imprisonment haunts whoever profited from Israel's genocidal oppression of the Palestinians for capitalist or political gains. Don't allow Zionist and imperial manipulations of reality to allow Israel to escape accountability and consolidate its domination of the Palestinian people and Arab lands.

We need poets, journalists, writers, artists, musicians, people to keep educating and creating for Palestine so the cause remains in people's consciousness until people are allowed to return and justice is served. No oppressive power ever surrendered voluntarily so we need to meet this escalating threat to humanity by escalating our efforts to save humanity, and take reassurance from history that, like South Africa's apartheid, Israel will be defeated.

I find direct action by unions blocking arms shipments to Israel or targeting the military and financial [companies] the most appropriate response. Direct-action groups shutting down arms factories or stopping companies involved in the genocide make me hopeful, and actionists have successfully shut down multiple factories in England and sustained millions in losses for Elbit Systems.

There needs to be more actions like these economy-disruptive actions like general strikes. Trade unions need to be more involved in Boycott, Divestment and Sanctions campaigns for there to be an impact on the economy. We need to target all aspects of the Israeli economy, and bring it to its knees.

Reach out to your Palestinian friends. Listen with empathy and spread the word in your community. Ensure that Palestinian voices are centred in debates involving their struggles and futures.

The last time we spoke in 2020 you warned that the situation was urgent. Do you think comrades heeded this call for urgency?

Yes, we warned people for years that it could lead to an explosive situation if Israel secured a pretext. Israel has already been carrying out massacres every few years while keeping Gaza under siege, making it completely unliveable.

I'm disappointed, so disappointed. Where are the academics that have made their careers on studying Indigenous cultures, settler colonialism, and Middle Eastern studies? Where are the feminists, the journalists, the medics, the lawyers, the unions? Even some solidarity campaigns fell into the trap of denouncing Palestinian resistance to Israel's occupation.

The people raving on October 7 were raving on stolen land, land that belongs to Palestinians right next to the world's largest concentration camp. This is where massacres were taking place before, yes *before*, October 7. Israel spread so many lies from what happened on that day, so much propaganda, but despite rigorous investigations that debunked all of their claims, they have stuck and have taken on a life of their own. Meanwhile, the massacres and ethnic cleansing and everything that has happened in Palestine for seventy-six years, what is happening right now in Gaza, doesn't carry the same weight.

It is the most televised massacre in history, it is happening live, but no power is interested in doing anything meaningful to stop it and business continues as usual. We are being dehumanised, over and over again. How much should Palestinians suffer? For how long? Why are we being left alone?

What is happening in Gaza doesn't just affect Palestinians, it affects all of us. It is affecting Lebanon and the whole of the Middle East. And what Israel is being allowed to get away with, its impunity, its crossing of red lines, it sets a precedent. Other governments will think they will be able to get away with genocide. Who knows what will happen.

How many times has it been repeated that the International Court of Justice has ruled that Israel is committing genocide, that Israel's occupation is illegal and needs to be stopped? And still, no one seems to be able to do anything to stop it because profit-oriented and racist sensibilities rule.

After the genocide, the times of governments and organisations trying to appease the Israeli government should be over. This reminds me of what happened with Jeremy Corbyn. When the UK finally had the chance of having a pro-Palestinian socialist leader, the British government didn't like it, and Israel didn't like it either, so he was accused of antisemitism and removed to appease Israel. But the genocide in Gaza shows us in full display how Israel's ideological conflation between anti-Zionism and antisemitism allows those accusers to go unchallenged. [Accusers who are themselves] accused of facilitating the biggest hoax in modern history to give Israel a pretext to mass exterminate and annihilate the Palestinians unchallenged.

Have you been approached by journalists; do you feel that your voice is heard and valued as a Palestinian living in the UK?

No. In a word, no. I don't feel heard. Not by mainstream media. I was approached for an interview with the BBC a while ago. I talked to the journalist about my family being killed and displaced in Gaza. One of their producers contacted me later thanking me for an important interview and reassuring me that they are waiting for an opportunity to release it, but they didn't even air the interview, rendering my emotional labour and time lost.

I was also approached by a woman from ITV [a British television channel] who was doing a report focusing on the impact of the genocide on children. I sent her pictures of my cousins' children who had been killed. In the end, she did a five-minute report. I watched her report again and again and nowhere did she say that it was Israel dropping the bombs that were killing the children.

I have been open to and welcomed opportunities to speak about my people whenever I have received any. Alternative media, such as Electronic Intifada, Palestine Deep Dive, Declassified UK, Breakthrough News, Novara Media, and Salam Media in South Africa, have been proactive in reporting silenced voices. But the mainstream media has always had its own agenda and is a tool facilitating this genocide. It starts with October 7, with no history or context, ignoring the fact that on October 6, Gaza was already widely known as an open-air prison.

You recently claimed a legal victory against your former employer, Sheffield Hallam University, whom you took to court for sharing confidential and derogatory information about you to the *Jewish Chronicle*. Does this victory feel more significant now?

Israel's ceaseless crimes overshadowed my capacity to celebrate my legal victory against my ex-employer, Sheffield Hallam University [in England].[1] This long-standing battle exposed the insidious application of the IHRA definition of antisemitism to demonise, harass, and silence Palestinian advocates and their supporters and reinforce Israel's impunity.[2]

It was terrible that an employer in UK higher education was allowed to do this to a Palestinian because Palestinians have so much to endure without being forced into these types of struggles. My story will hopefully give a warning for other employers harassing their employees for opposing Israel and help other victims to fight similar cases and win.

The European Legal Support Centre and my local unions supported me, enabling me to win twice. No one should be intimidated, and people should feel reassured that speaking the truth and opposing injustice should not be career suicide. There are mechanisms and networks that can offer support if someone finds themselves in a crisis.

Whatever we sacrifice by speaking up though, is nothing compared to a child losing his life under the rubble of his home or being imprisoned in Israeli jails.

I saw this quote recently from Antonio Gramsci: 'The old world is dying, and the new world struggles to be born: now is the time of monsters.' This is true, this is the time of monsters. They are all collaborating to reinforce their gains before they allow us a chance to bury our martyrs. But it is also the time for all people of conscience, from all walks of life, to collaborate to dismantle capitalism and colonialism.

---

1 Simon Childs, 'A Palestinian Academic Thought Her Ordeal with Her Employer Was Over. Then It 'Reached Out to the *Jewish Chronicle*', Novara Media, November 4, 2024, https://novaramedia.com/2024/11/04/a-palestinian-academic-thought-her-ordeal-with-her-employer-was-over-then-it-reached-out-to-the-jewish-chronicle.

2 The International Holocaust Remembrance Alliance's definition of antisemitism has been widely criticised for conflating antisemitism and criticism of Israel and silencing those who stand in solidarity with Palestinians.

Sireen Khudairy

Sireen is from Tubas in the northern Jordan Valley. She is currently living in Dheisheh refugee camp in Bethlehem in the West Bank. Throughout her life Sireen has been an organiser against the colonisation of the Jordan Valley. She came to live in Dheisheh in 2015 after meeting her husband, Mahmoud. We interviewed Sireen in August 2018 at her home.

Can you tell us about your youth?
I was born in 1987 during the First Intifada [the name given for the popular uprising that took place in Palestine from 1987 to 1991], and grew up in the town of Tubas which is close to the north of the Jordan Valley. Lots of people in Tubas own land in the Jordan Valley and work there as farmers, agricultural labourers, or shepherds.

Before 1967, people used to go from Tubas to their land in the Jordan Valley by walking through the mountains. Now they have to go through a checkpoint—sometimes it's open and sometimes not. The soldiers search people and it's a problem for the farmers because they have to wait with their fresh produce at the checkpoints, sometimes for hours.

During the Second Intifada—from 2000 to 2005—it was hard to go into the Jordan Valley without a permit. During that time we used to walk around the Al-Hamra checkpoint [in defiance of the Israeli restrictions]. It is Israeli policy to separate the Palestinian people in the West Bank from the valley.

My family has land in the village of Bardala, planted with guava. My dad used to live in Bardala, but at that time there were no schools in the Jordan Valley so he took the easier solution and decided to move, which is what the occupation wanted. When I got older I wondered why people had taken the easier way out and moved away.

When I was young I went to visit a relative in Al-Maleh in the north of the Jordan Valley. It was the first time I had been there. I returned home feeling totally sick. The people in Al-Maleh didn't have water or electricity. They lived in a very bad situation. After that, I started to ask my father more about the situation in the Jordan Valley. I was thirteen years old then.

He explained to me then about Area C.[1] I complained to my parents, 'Why did you hide your experiences of life in the Jordan Valley from us? Why did you wait until I asked you about the real situation there before you explained it to me?'

In 2005 I got involved in Jordan Valley Solidarity (JVS) [a Palestinian campaign against the Israeli colonisation of the valley]. I joined them to help with translation and it was an opportunity for me to learn more from the people. I did tours for internationals who had come in solidarity and I worked as a project coordinator.

The main goal of Jordan Valley Solidarity is to support the existence of people in the Jordan Valley through different activities, for example, through rebuilding houses [that have been demolished by the occupation]. We managed to build five different schools and five health centres in Area C and we laid water pipes into three different communities.

You were arrested by Israeli occupation forces. Can you tell us what happened?

In 2013, on the anniversary of the Nakba,[2] I was arrested. The arrest was a big surprise. I was on my way back from university. A flying military checkpoint had been set up in Tubas and they stopped my car and the other cars on the road.[3] I was feeling fine, not expecting

1 The majority of the valley was designated Area C under the 1993 Oslo Accords, meaning that the area would be under Israeli control until the establishment of a Palestinian state. Of course, the Israeli regime never allowed the formation of a Palestinian state, but Area C remained as a zone of control. Since then Israel has forbidden Palestinians from building any structures in Area C, or from developing water or electric infrastructure. The occupation forces bulldoze anything that Palestinians build.

2 *Nakba*, meaning 'catastrophe', is the Palestinian name for the ethnic cleansing of 1947–49, and is marked every May 15.

3 Flying checkpoints are temporary roadblocks, set up to control Palestinian people's movement, or to detain people.

anything. They demanded our IDs, and then they asked me to get out of the car. After fifteen minutes an officer said to me, 'You are arrested.' He bound my hands and blindfolded me. I asked him if he had an official paper [authorising my arrest], but he refused to answer.

Later, youths who were on the mountains above us started to throw stones at the checkpoint. The officer put me in front of him and put his gun on my shoulder and started shooting at the stone throwers with the gun balanced on me. He was using me as a human shield. It was so scary. For two weeks afterwards I wasn't able to hear properly.

Then they took me to a military base—I guess—I'm not sure as I was blindfolded. I could only see lots of Israeli feet and shoes on the ground beneath my eyes. They arrested me at 2.00pm and they kept me in the military base on a tiny concrete bench for hours. I wasn't allowed to drink anything or go to the toilet. Each time the soldiers passed me, they came close to my ear, shouted at me and prepared their weapons as if they were going to shoot.

They took me from the military base at around 2.00am. Then they put me on a bus full of soldiers, still blindfolded, but I could see a little from the bottom of the blindfold. It was scary on the bus with those soldiers and their shouting. They were saying bad words to me, and calling me 'Arab', saying 'Arabs are animals' and 'you are just an Arab woman.' Another soldier said 'Arab women are very cheap. If I wanted, I could sleep with you.'

An Israeli captain for Tubas area came to me and said, 'We are on our way to your parents' house. I want you to tell us where your personal stuff is, like your laptop, camera, and notebook.' He threatened me that if I didn't give them this stuff they would make things hard for my parents. We arrived at my parents' house and they took two laptops, a camera, my phone, and notebooks from my room. My mum asked them if she could see me but they refused. They stayed in my parents' house for around two or three hours, making a mess.

People started to throw stones at the military vehicle I was in (they didn't know that I was inside), so the army responded by shooting tear gas and live bullets. They shot one of my friends and because of that he lost four fingers. Then they took me into isolation at Al-Jalameh prison [near Haifa, inside the Green Line].

I was kept there for one month in a cell which was one metre wide and two metres long. There was a toilet inside. I had no window and there was only a very small orange light. The military interrogated me for ten hours per day, maybe more. The only way I could see the time was when they put the food under the door, and then I could see the watch on the soldier's wrist. That's the only way I could keep track of the date, and the only way that I knew it was a new day.

In the first week of my interrogation there was a big chair, on which they asked me questions for ten or eleven hours. They plugged me into a lie detector. And they told me that it said I was lying. They asked me about Jordan Valley Solidarity, and whether I was in a leftist party. They were interrogating me about my friends and family, and then questioned me more deeply, for example about the filming of a documentary called *The Last Shepherd in the Jordan Valley*. I was surprised that they knew the journalists in the film. They asked me how we had managed to meet the Israeli settlers who we had interviewed.

I demanded the right to meet with my lawyer. But they only allowed me to see him after I had been imprisoned for forty days. Other questions that they asked were about the photos on my laptop, about what I was thinking about doing in the future, if I planned on threatening Israeli security. They were very sure that I was planning something and they wanted to know what the plan was. They tried to make lots of pressure against me. They gave me fake news, for example that my mother had had to go to hospital after the raid on the house. They said to me that my dad had said in a newspaper that I had shamed the family.

After one month in isolation, they brought in a guy who said he was from Tubas, my hometown, to the cell next to mine. There was a hole in the wall, which was supposed to be a drain for water, and we could talk through this hole. This guy said to me, 'I'm really sorry but I told them about our plan to kill Israelis.' When he said that I reacted in a very harsh way. I said, 'What are you talking about? Which plan?' In one second the door of the cell was opened and the captain was sitting next to him to see if I was lying. The captain said, 'Okay, now we trust you that you're not going to kill Israelis. Now you can take rest and tomorrow you will go to court.'

The judge in the court said to me that they have decided to send me to Hasharon prison [between Tulkarem in the occupied West Bank, and Netanya inside the Green Line] but that before I went there, they would send me to isolation in Ashkelon prison for two days. They told me they were preparing my place in Hasharon. But actually, it was a trick to make me think that I was going to be safer, and that I would be with other Palestinian prisoners.

There was another Palestinian who they wanted me to trust, and he told me that he had a secret phone in the jail. He asked me if I wanted to talk to my mother. I decided to give him a fake phone number. When he came back and said that he had spoken to my mother I knew that he must be a spy. Later the same man came back again and told me that my 'comrades outside jail' would take care of me and that they 'needed me to answer some questions' so that they could support me. The questions were about whether I was in the Popular Front for the Liberation of Palestine (PFLP). The questionnaire had a fake stamp on it that said PFLP. I couldn't tell him that I knew he was a spy because a few months before, a Palestinian man called Arafat Jaradat had confronted a spy in prison, and [Arafat] had been killed.[4]

I stayed in Ashkelon for one week, and then they took me back to Al-Jalameh, to the same captain. He was very angry and he slapped me. There were nine people in the room surrounding me, half of them were shouting at me. Two of them were kicking my chair. This happened for about four hours. After that, they interrogated me for three more days. Five days later I was sent to Hasharon prison.

Sireen was imprisoned for three months in total on that occasion. She was released after her family paid 7,000 Israeli shekels for her release.[5] *Her release was conditional on Sireen staying at her family's home. She was forbidden from using the internet, thus isolating her from all but her immediate family and preventing her from continuing her studies. She was ordered to return to court on September 16, 2013, where she was found not guilty of Israel's trumped-up charges. But the court still ordered her not to engage in any political activity for five years.*

How did you feel when you were released from prison?

After the experience of jail I was thinking about stopping my work with JVS. I remember talking to a friend at the time, and they said

4 To learn more about the death of Arafat Jaradat see Talia Ralph, MintPress, February 25, 2013, https://www.mintpressnews.com/arafat-jaradat-palestinian-prisoner-dies-in-israeli-jail/51292.

5 Seven thousand Israeli shekels are roughly equivalent to 1,966 US dollars or 1,727 euros, depending on the exchange rate.

to me, 'The occupation could destroy your house, they could put you in prison, but something they can't destroy is your hope. If they do manage to destroy your hope that means you are occupied. If they don't manage it, you are above the occupation.'

So I started studying theatre, and presenting stories through drama with the ASHTAR theatre group. Our technique is called the Theatre of the Oppressed. Our first project was to educate Palestinian youths working in the Israeli settlements in the Jordan Valley. There were seven young people, aged from twenty-two to twenty-seven. Most of them were working in the settlements and it was an opportunity for them to share stories about their lives, to learn theatre, and to work because we gave opportunities for people to be employees at ASHTAR theatre.

ASHTAR would perform a story, and then invite the audience to rewrite the story with the solution. The idea was to invite the Palestinian Authority as well, and for the politicians to put themselves in the place of the oppressed. We would write down the solutions that the audiences came up with, and we would organise conferences where we would talk strategically about these solutions. So it's not just about presenting stories, it's about getting solutions from people, to get ideas to build a strategy and work on it.

One positive outcome of our performances was that there was an official permit granted to open a school for five different communities in the Jordan Valley, but unfortunately the governor died before it could happen.

You were arrested two more times, once by the Israeli occupation and once by the Palestinian Authority. What happened?

The Palestinian Authority detained me for a day in December 2013, and psychologically they treated me worse than the Israelis. Or maybe it just felt worse because I felt that they should be my people. They were talking to me like I was an enemy, saying that they 'had a peace agreement with Israel', and that I should 'respect this agreement'.

That time I was detained in Tubas, my hometown. In Tubas it is very shameful to arrest a woman, and I think that's the reason why they didn't hold me longer. They said to me that the Israelis were 'going to arrest me again soon' if I carried on [opposing the occupation] and that I should 'take care of this shitty business'.

In January 2014 I was arrested again by the Israeli military, in Nablus. They took me to Huwara [where there is an Israeli military base and checkpoint, just outside Nablus]. The soldiers took off my jacket and shoes and the Israeli commander said to me that I should remember that 'I was under occupation by the only democratic state in the Middle East' and that they were going to teach me how to respect Israel. When I heard this I went crazy, and I said, 'It's not democracy; it's a criminal state. You are using this "democracy" to kick people out of their houses and make people homeless.'

The commander was really angry. He told me to run. My feet were tied and my hands too. As well as my shoes, they had even taken off my socks. The ground was covered in sharp stones. The soldiers released dogs and they started to run at me. I felt pain in my feet from stepping on the sharp stones. When the soldiers caught up with me they started hitting me on the shoulders with their weapons. When I was released most of my body was blue.

I had never been scared of dogs before, but that night I saw that the dogs were under the control of the soldiers and they were capable of anything. Since then, I'm scared if I see a dog. Much later, I was with an international woman in the Jordan Valley, giving her a tour and explaining the situation. She didn't know much about Palestine. Suddenly I saw a dog and I was really scared. She didn't understand why I was so scared. She started to blame my culture and background. I realised that international people need to learn more about our culture. If you don't understand the people, then you can't be part of our struggle.

After the beating, they kept me under arrest for four days. They kept me in a military vehicle and took me to court twice. They didn't allow me to sleep for two days. In fact, they had just arrested me so they could give me a beating, but I was thinking that they were going to keep me for a long time. They threatened that they could keep me for years.

After this arrest Sireen met her husband Mahmoud, and moved to Dheisheh to be with him. But before long Mahmoud was also arrested. What happened to Mahmoud?

In 2015 I got married and moved here to Dheisheh. My husband Mahmoud was an ex-prisoner too and, before we were married, the Israeli captain, who was called Captain Nidal—'governor of

Dheisheh'—threatened Mahmoud. He told Mahmoud that the two of us would never get married and stay in one house together.[6]

One month after we were married, me and my husband travelled to Jordan. I was planning to be part of three theatre performances there. But the Israeli authorities stopped us at the border for four hours. The commander came and asked to talk to Mahmoud for ten minutes, but actually they arrested him, and he was in prison for a year. I went to Jordan and then went back to Palestine to go to his court case. They sentenced Mahmoud to one year for joining a demonstration, where they said that he threw rocks and molotovs. Mahmoud had been in jail before, but he had been released because of a negotiated amnesty. They were threatening to put him back in prison for the remainder of his previous sentence. But the lawyer negotiated and luckily this didn't happen.

I had only moved to Dheisheh two months before Mahmoud was arrested. When Mahmoud was in prison I was living here alone. It was difficult, because I thought that any night the army could come and attack the camp. But I wanted to stay there to show that I would not run away. It wasn't easy to keep on living there. With each attack in Dheisheh I thought that they would come for me.

The army attacks Dheisheh often. It isn't easy for them to enter Dheisheh [because of the resistance], but recently they have started to use the strategy of dressing up like Palestinian citizens and entering Dheisheh with cars that have Palestinian plates. Whenever they're in Dheisheh you feel like you're in a war. They use sound bombs, tear gas, and shoot automatic rifles. You can hear shouting and Palestinian people being injured. I often hear injured people screaming in pain or pleading for an ambulance. They attack and arrest people from the street. Sometimes they detain people and blindfold them and leave them in the street for hours.

---

6 An Arabic-speaking agent from the Israeli Shin Bet security services using the alias 'Captain Nidal' has made more than one threat to people in Dheisheh. According to a 2016 article by Nora Barrows-Freedman in *Electronic Intifada*, Palestinian youth have testified that Captain Nidal told them, 'I will make all the youth of the camp disabled', 'I will have all of you walking with crutches and in wheelchairs', 'I will make half of you disabled, and let the other half push the wheelchairs', and 'I will make all of you stand in line at the ATM waiting for your disability subsidies and assistance.' See Nora Barrows-Friedman, 'Israeli Captain: "I Will Make You All Disabled"', *Electronic Intifada*, September 1, 2016, https://electronicintifada.net/content/israeli-captain-i-will-make- you-all-disabled/17821.

The army often comes and attacks the camp at 1.00am or 2.00am, but recently they have started coming at 5.00am or 6.00am. They want to break the resistance, because even now the people keep resisting. Whenever the army attacks, people resist. The women throw shoes at the army when they come to attack our homes. The Palestinian Authority's security forces also attack the camp and arrest people. For example, Mahmoud was in a Palestinian jail for a month and a half.

Before moving to Dheisheh I used to hear people talking about the resistance in the camp. It was my dream to visit Dheisheh. When I put my feet in Dheisheh I felt like I was a tree, and that my roots were going deep under the streets of Dheisheh. I felt for the first time that I was in a very rich place. Although I didn't know many people, I remember hearing the voices of the people in the houses while I was walking on the streets and that gave me warmth. I felt close to the people there.

I like the way that the people here stand with each other. How they still feel connected to each other. For example, if someone is wanted for arrest, even if most of the people know where he is, he feels safe. He or she could receive help from many different people. I love the way that people cooperate with each other. That's what's most touched me—that people have solidarity with each other. They support each other because they like to do it, not because they have to.

People here accepted me into the community and they called me 'the lady of the village'. They were very excited to learn about planting trees, and what it feels like to live in a village. The key for me was to talk about the Jordan Valley. The people here are very educated, but they don't know about life in the Jordan Valley.

While I was living in Dheisheh, me and a friend decided to establish an art residency in the village of Fasayil in the Jordan Valley. During the residency we visited families, sharing life and sitting with the women, asking them what they did with their lives and what they wanted to do. In the beginning they used to answer that they did nothing. But when we went deeper, we realised that they woke up at 4.00am to milk hundreds of sheep, they prepared their children for school, they milked the sheep in the afternoon, they did homework for the kids.

They worked from 4.00am until 9.00pm doing hard work. But for them this was 'nothing'. If there is a house demolition [by the Israeli military], the first people who take the stuff out of the house are the women. If the bulldozers come, the women will still make food for their sons and daughters. They build new houses, ready to live in again. These women have power, but they don't feel that they have it. Visiting those women was like going to school, a school where we learned about the meaning of hope and power.

Another part of my and my friend's project was to show the beauty of the Jordan Valley—the birds, the space, the peacefulness, the unique plants, and the mountains. In the future we want to organise a walk for women from all over Palestine so that they can hear the stories [of the people from the valley] and their beautiful memories from the area. The activities will be led by women. Another of our aims is to learn traditional Arabic culture through exchanging cultural experiences, through daily life. Making mud bricks for building houses, training, and planting, and working in the fields.

There is a refugee camp in the Jordan Valley called Abu Al Ajaj camp. The people who live there are the families of people who fled from their homes in 1967 [after the Israeli occupation of the West Bank]. What's happening in Abu Al-Ajaj is still an ongoing Nakba [catastrophe]. We as Palestinians should have learnt from what happened to the refugees of 1948, but we didn't. It happened again in 1967. We didn't learn the lesson either that time. We still live in an ongoing Nakba, where the Israeli army is destroying houses and moving people from one place to another place. We should start to build connections between Dheisheh camp and Abu Al Ajaj, to give an opportunity for people in Abu Al Ajaj to have connections with people in Dheisheh.

We have to sit with the old people to know the real stories, to know why things are as they are, and to build strategies. People can be pushed from the Jordan Valley at any time. We need strategies to stop this.

You want to establish a women's centre in Dheisheh?

The idea of the women's centre is to make a dead place alive again. Mahmoud's family owns an old house. It's one of the oldest places in Dheisheh, four generations of people have lived there. It belongs to Mahmoud's aunt who lives in Jordan now. We want to renovate it. In the meantime, we're having meetings as a small group of women in our houses.

When Mahmoud was in jail, he received a monthly salary from the Palestinian Authority. [Historically, they paid a monthly stipend for Palestinians held in Israeli jails. As of May 2025, this fund has largely been scrapped.] We collected that money and decided to do this project for the community. We will call it Dar Siti [my grandma's house].

It will be a place for friends to stay, for studying, and a meeting place. Dar Siti will be based on the 'grandmother style' of living, with the traditional style of sitting on the floor, and cooking in the way that our grandmothers cooked. We want to reclaim our old culture, the old ways of living. Dar Siti will be a place for activists and artists to be closer to the community, to talk to them, and to build their work together.

The women of Dheisheh are organising social activities for the families of prisoners and martyred people, and they're also organising protests to support prisoners. We all try to sit and talk together about our different situations. That's really important. Women's organising is very strong in Dheisheh now.

Sireen's husband Mahmoud was arrested in the wave of repression across the West Bank which followed Israel's 2023 attack on the Gaza Strip. He has remained in administrative detention without charge for almost two years.

Lama Suleiman

Lama is from Haifa, inside the Green Line. She grew up in Nazareth and has since lived in the UK and studied in London. After returning from the UK, Lama continued her studies as a postgraduate student in Haifa. She talks about how anarchism and feminism have influenced her. We interviewed Lama in August 2018, at her home in Haifa.

What was your experience of attending an Israeli university?
Throughout my experience of studying in Israeli universities, I was often the only Palestinian in the programme. I encountered systemic discrimination on a daily basis, but having the privilege of getting a foreign education [in the UK] had put me at a higher level than Israeli students and enabled me to overcome the very stark educational disadvantages that limited my work and my access to knowledge.

The experience of alienation also extended to my encounters with students and peers. I was always the Arab that didn't fit their stereotypes, but when it came to my Palestinian identity or academic work, they were at best uncomfortable topics, and at worst, belligerently discredited by my Israeli peers for not conforming to their hegemonic narratives and values.

Can you talk about how ideas of non-hierarchy influenced you while you were at university in London?
I learnt a lot of things that have stuck with me from my experience of the anarchist movement in the UK. Especially ideas about non-hierarchy, because this helps you understand your place in a movement, your relationship to others, and the emotions that you have being part of a group.

Dealing with these emotions and ideas in a group is a strong aspect of how you can sustain deep activism and build community. It's one of the most important building blocks of creating a sustainable radical left movement. I was quite young at the time, and I found this experience to have inspired much of my work, activism, and writing.

Unfortunately, after being active in Palestine for the past seven to eight years, the difficulties, power relations, and inner tensions I have encountered within the Palestinian community in Haifa have really drained my energies.

Did this influence you when you returned to Palestine?

When I came back here, I wanted to utilise anarchist ideas and methods in the place that I know best. But I didn't really succeed, for many different reasons. In my immediate circle in Haifa, I found that people weren't very interested in talking about group dynamics or power relations. They were mostly preoccupied with the larger context of Israeli oppression and occupation, and social hierarchies were not perceived as an important thing to struggle against. I think that's a shame, and counterproductive.

But I've always believed that things have to develop organically. I think you can learn a lot from other struggles but I don't think you can simply import ideas from other places and expect people to practise them. Yet, since the last couple of years a more radical feminist and queer discourse has been developing in Palestine.

How would you describe your politics now?

I don't agree with using labels when talking about politics; I think politics should be a conversation. The only label I would identify with and try to live by here is the label 'feminist'. It's the most immediate and daily struggle for me. I don't consider myself a Palestinian nationalist, but I identify as a Palestinian as an anti-colonial political identity. I couldn't call myself an anti-capitalist either, because I have been habituated to being a consumer. I would consider myself to be an anarchist. Yet, while I abstain from dealing with Israeli colonial institutions, my livelihood is often dependent on the state. And although I think the parliamentary system (especially in Israel) is an illusion of democracy, sometimes voting for Palestinians can be tactical.

However, to be an anarchist, you can't live a radical life on your own, you need a community of people around you in order to develop. I don't think that I live my life the way I believe in right now. I have reached a point where I have to conform to the way things are in order to get things done. There aren't many loopholes in the way of life here; you can't really escape the system. Life is too integrated into capitalism, and Israel is one of the strongest capitalist systems in the Western world today, even more so than the UK.

Also, the path I have chosen, writing and researching, means I have to be in an academic framework to do it, and following that path has meant that I am integrated into the capitalist system. My daily life here is struggling to pay rent, so it doesn't leave me that much space. But I guess that's just how it is in any capitalist country.

Can you talk about people's struggle to survive financially here in Haifa?

Israel is supposedly a welfare state. It's built on the premise of a welfare state [i.e., high taxation]. But your taxes go toward paying for the military apparatus of the state and to serve the interests of corporations and wealthy sectors. The system only supports you if you're on or below the poverty line, and even then you get the bare minimum to survive so you can continue to exist in a state of perpetual poverty and debt.

The system in the UK is better able to absorb changes in the economy than in Israel. Here there is a lot more precariousness. A lot of young people here are unemployed, and rely on temporary and precarious jobs with unlawful work and pay conditions. There aren't [many] unions to support precarious workers.[1] And it is common for employers to take advantage of their workers especially because there aren't many work opportunities available to them elsewhere.

In the last two years [2016–18], the economy has been changing, the rents have been steadily rising, but salaries have stayed the same and are below what you need to get by. I'm now thirty-three years old with a master's degree, but I can't get a job to live on or develop from.

1 MAAN is one union that works with precarious Palestinian workers within the Green Line. See http://eng.wac-maan.org.il.

How does Israeli capitalism intersect with Israel's colonisation of Palestine?

The Israeli settler project and the other Western colonialist projects in the Middle East were never really about nationalism. Zionist colonialism has been a capitalist colonial project since it began in the 1900s. Although Palestine has historically been a capitalist society, nowadays it is reliant on the Israeli occupation and its economy, and the Palestinian Authority (PA) is itself complicit in producing and perpetuating capitalist relations and inequalities.

Can you talk a little bit about why you don't identify as a Palestinian nationalist?

The Palestinian predicament for the last hundred years is the result of nationalism eclipsing anti-colonialism, which was a much more inclusive struggle. Historically the struggle was never about Palestinian nationalism. I think Palestinian nationalism was a reaction to Zionist immigration and to the Jewish nationalist project. Palestinian nationalist discourse began as a strategic discourse to counter it. Nationalism was growing at the time. So in some ways it was the only language that people could take up. Nationalism was the only way for the Arabs in Palestine to stand their ground and claim their entitlement to their land.

The more history has unfolded, the stronger the nationalist discourse has grown. There were a lot of different ideas that we have lost along the way. A similar process happened in the UK, in Europe. Just like everywhere else, nationalism had won. I think the turning point was the Zionist immigration [to Palestine] and the victory of the nationalist discourse. It doesn't mean that all the ideas that came before were lost. There are still echoes even now in certain places. The ethnic cleansing of 1948 also had a significant effect in completely disconnecting what was before and what came after.

What do you think were the ideas lost along the way? Before there was nationalism, what were people's ideas?

Before the end of the Ottoman Empire, there were a lot of people talking about the decentralisation of the empire. There was talk about all of the different Arab, non-Arab, and various religious communities across the empire having equal rights, and becoming citizens of the empire. There were discussions about decentralising power from Istanbul, and for every region of the empire to have its own autonomy.

There were Islamic discourses too, and there were also Arab nationalists, who sought to create a pan-Arab state. What is going on today in Syria with ISIS is not so detached from these two discourses. It's a continuation of what was disrupted along the way. There was a huge spectrum of ideas. Some ideas stick, some don't.

I don't consider myself a Palestinian nationalist at heart. But I would think of myself as a Palestinian nationalist politically speaking, in terms of how I would identify myself, in order to counter Israeli racism and colonial discourses. So it's more of a strategic thing for me.

Would you be happy to see a Palestinian state emerge?

That's a difficult question. But I don't think that there will really be a Palestinian state. [A Palestinian state] already exists in some form and I don't think anyone really likes how it looks. So it wouldn't be a desirable state for the future. I don't believe in a two-state solution and I don't believe that a one-state solution is possible any more. Even though the latter is the most ideal, it is already past the point where it's possible to achieve.

Personally, I think that Palestinian identity can only exist theoretically. When the Great March of Return began in Gaza [in 2018], I was closed up in my room for a few months and I was reading and writing for my research about Palestinian history. At the time, I was really detached from reality, because what I was researching was pre-1948, and it has a lot of nostalgia and magic in it.

I began thinking about the Great March of Return in Gaza, I started connecting it to what I had been reading, and I started to see that people participating in the march still have that nostalgic vision of Palestine, and aren't willing to let go of it. They still thought that it was a place to which they *can* return. That realisation had a lot of sadness in it. The marchers are attached to returning to somewhere that doesn't exist anymore.

We Palestinians inside Israel know this very well. There is nothing left here. We try to symbolically say 'Yes! We remained in Haifa', and we are doing these cultural projects to reclaim the Palestinian heritage of the city but we know hardly any of it really exists anymore. It is only in our imaginations. This idea that young people in Gaza are willing to die for something that deep down they know doesn't exist anymore, it only goes to show the level of despair we have come to.

Here [as Palestinians living within the Green Line] we are in denial about most things. We keep ourselves to ourselves, we try to make the most of the everyday and we try to avoid violence and immediate conflict. We try to live life normally. While in other parts of Palestine, life is anything but normal. But we're still really attached to this idea of Palestine. So how do you reconcile nationalism, and wanting a state, wanting to better the lives of people who have been suffering for decades—how do you reconcile this with the fact that what they want doesn't exist anymore? Maybe this way of thinking has to do with where we are. Living in Haifa, in the north, in what many refer to as 'historic Palestine'.

How much have you heard about the Kurdish freedom movement and the revolution in Rojava: the idea of democratic confederalism and people organising in a directly democratic way at local street level?

The Kurdish freedom movement was calling for a state. They were nationalist in the same way that Palestinian movements are. But then they began to call for democratic confederalism instead of a state, and they began to criticise states as just another form of oppression. How much do people in Palestine know about this? I don't think people know enough about it at all. I think that the Kurdish situation is a common reference point that is similar to the Palestinian crisis in many ways. But I don't think our situations have been compared that much.

I think the Kurdish freedom movement today has managed to succeed in doing what the Palestinians didn't. It's a good example of anti-nationalism, and that's the main difference to the Palestinian struggle. They succeeded despite not having the privilege of having the world's attention—at least not until recently. I think we could learn a lot from that, if we would listen.

For Palestinians the struggle against colonialism and capitalism is very much concentrated on the Israeli occupation. Unless we break out of that framework we won't be able to accomplish much. The world has become so woven together, I don't think that you can separate one issue from another anymore. Being occupied by Israel diverts our attention from places where we can make change. The Israeli state isn't going to collapse any time soon, it is what it is. Just like capitalism isn't going to disappear in one day. It's part of the same logic.

As long as the nationalist struggle is only focused on anti-Zionism, it is just a reaction specifically against Israel, then it doesn't have much potential to change the smaller things. The things that get forgotten but which are of no lesser importance. For example, I think community building is crucial. I think institution building is not possible inside the Israeli state: there are too many laws against it. Although, there is much more possibility within the Palestinian state.

You talked about feminism earlier, and self-identified as a feminist. Can you talk about what it's like to be a Palestinian feminist inside the Israeli state?

There are different experiences of being a feminist here in different frameworks. It's different if you're a Palestinian woman in an Israeli institution or, for example, a woman living in a Palestinian village, or a Palestinian woman living in an Israeli city—these factors change your experiences greatly. And then there's also the issue of being a woman within the private sphere of the family. For me at least, I take on different feminist identities in each of these frameworks. The most problematic sphere for me is the private sphere, where I feel I have to compromise my own values and way of life in order to keep the peace and not to insult anyone. Whereas when I am in public I don't really care what people think, and I don't worry about the outcomes, as they don't affect me as much.

In Haifa, I can say and dress how I like because people don't know me here. In Nazareth where my family live it would be different and I would have to change my appearance and behaviour to adapt to the value system of the place. I would have to think twice about what I'm wearing, how I speak, and where I'm going. I don't come from a traditional family but I still encounter some situations where I'm not accepted as I am, and I am expected to change or compromise in order to please the rest of the family. It is a choice of whether to confront or to keep the peace. It's something I have to keep thinking about, about where to draw the line between when to compromise—to keep the peace—and when I have to enter into a confrontation in order to protect my personal space or to fight for something I really want/need. It's kind of weird that after [more than] thirty years of living I'm still not used to it. Maybe someday I will be.

Could you talk about feminist organising inside Israel, and in Palestinian society in general?

Well I've never been active in feminist organising in Palestine before. I think most of the feminist organisations here are traditional in the sense that they operate only within the gaps left by the Israeli state, in the places where people fall between the cracks. In most cases feminist organising has to do with violence against women, focusing on violence in the family, honour killings, forced marriages, etc. But I have rarely encountered organisations that work on sexual harassment in the workplace, which is one of the most prevalent problems that women encounter here on a day-to-day basis.

I think feminist organisations have the potential to grow here if they include women who have different kinds of experiences, to validate and affirm these experiences and differences, and to move away from discourses of victimisation. Feminism in Palestine is not yet intersectional enough as it does not discuss/mobilise around other issues/inequalities such as class, or queer, or racial discrimination within Palestinian society. [Palestinian queer organisation] alQaws, for example, is another progressive and radical organisation in Palestine that has been developing a very interesting queer-relevant discourse and practice. They have clear feminist overtones, but it too has not been very open to considering intersectional action.

I think that as long as different Palestinian movements and struggles remain limited to identity politics, the more time it will take us to begin to make important connections between discourses, movements, actions, and struggles.

Do you think nationalism has limited the space available for struggles against patriarchy and LGBTQI+ struggles?

Actually, I think the nationalist struggle does have space for feminist discourse and for other struggles. Both nationalist and feminist discourses can exist together, I think they come together quite nicely. They bring out the importance of anti-colonialism. It's an interesting question, especially when it comes to struggles around sexuality. A friend on Facebook recently asked a question about whether there are any stories in Palestinian folklore that mention queer sexuality. It's definitely a matter worth researching, and I am sure some have already begun doing so.

What are your thoughts on radical organising in Palestine?

The Palestine Liberation Organisation (PLO) was formed during the military rule [in Israel from 1948 to 1966] in the first two decades after the Nakba. But this wasn't the beginning of the Palestinian struggle; there were many significant Palestinian anti-colonial movements before that.

During the 1920s there were big Arab mobilisations here in Haifa, in Jerusalem, Nazareth, and other cities, by workers' labour unions and women's movements. This was in the context of the growing consciousness of the threat of Zionist immigration, and the ways it was affecting the Palestinian economy, agriculture, and industrial development, as well as the British policies that were accommodating Zionist immigration and institution building and causing a Palestinian recession.

People were also increasingly aware of the vast class inequalities within Arab society and communities in Palestine, and the ways in which rich Arab capitalists were complicit in the oppression of the working class, and the British colonial policies in Haifa and other cities and villages.

What about nationalism and the anti-colonial struggle?

The struggle began as an anti-colonial struggle in the late nineteenth century and early twentieth century, but after World War II anti-colonialism and anti-capitalism became sidelined by nationalism. The nationalist movement took form in a number of ways. Even before World War I, Palestinian nationalist movements were beginning to develop. Their development has a lot to do with 'Arab modernity', which was similar to Western modernity in the industrial sense, but culturally Arab modernity was quite different.

The concept of Arab modernity developed towards the end of the nineteenth century. The 1930s and 1940s were the height of Arab modernity—with the development of theatre, of photography, of political mobilisation, and feminist mobilisation. A Palestinian philanthropist living in East Jerusalem founded the Arab Bank.[2] The Arab Bank was an attempt to create an autonomous bank for people here not to rely on foreign institutions. Yet, the breaking up of Greater Syria also meant that modernity took different forms in Syria and Lebanon than it took in Palestine.

2 The Arab Bank, founded in Jerusalem in 1930, was the first private financial institution in the Arab world. It is now headquartered in Amman, Jordan.

Shrouq Aila

Shrouq is from Jabalia refugee camp, in northern Gaza. She is currently displaced to Deir al Balah, in central Gaza. Shrouq has been working as a journalist following the killing of her journalist husband, Roshdi Sarraj, by an Israeli air strike in October 2023. We interviewed Shrouq between December 12, 2024, and January 1, 2025, via WhatsApp voice notes.

Can you tell us about where you grew up in Gaza and where you have been displaced to since?
I grew up in Jabalia refugee camp, which is in the far north of the Gaza Strip. It has been totally under military siege for two to three months and they are suffering from heavy bombardment and ground invasions. Every day there are massacres. They are slaughtering the people in Jabalia.

Roshdi was from Gaza City so we got married there and stayed in Gaza City but close to the shore, by the sea; it is ten minutes by car from Jabalia. You have to know that the entire Gaza Strip is just one hour from the far south to the far north; it is very small. So moving from one area to the other is usually not a big deal because it's just a few minutes by car. For example, now I'm in Deir al Balah, in the centre of the Gaza Strip. I'm just ten minutes away from my home in the north, but I cannot go because of that military separation [the Netzarim Corridor] between the north and the south.

After they bombed Roshdi's family's house in October 2023, I moved to my sister's home in Jabalia. Then they bombed the next-door neighbours' house and it collapsed on us, so we were pulled out from under the rubble once again. That morning we decided to leave because there were no homes left for us in the north, all of them were destroyed.

We moved to Rafah, which is in the far south of the Gaza Strip. We were hosted there for almost six months at one of my relative's homes, in their apartment. It was very small, it consisted of two rooms. The men slept in the living room, the women and kids in the other room. We slept with almost nineteen people in one room. But this was a home; there were walls to protect you from the cold.

When the Rafah invasion started, we then moved to Deir al Balah, which is in the centre of the Gaza Strip. Deir al Balah is a very small city, smaller than [Khan] Younis, smaller than Gaza City, smaller than Rafah. Now 90 percent of Khan Younis has been destroyed after the Israeli army launched a military invasion there, which has been going on for almost seven months. They destroyed all the houses and even the standing ones are partially destroyed. So [Khan] Younis is now full of tents, it's the land of tents and crowds.

We stayed in a tent in Deir al Balah as we had no option to move to a house; the standing buildings were very few. We lived in the tent for almost six months. We just moved at the beginning of October 2024, which is the beginning of winter. Eventually we found an apartment so we are renting it, and now we are just waiting to go back to the north.

What is life like for you and your daughter surviving genocide? What was life like before?

We are surviving but it is not something that we manage to do, it's just the life that we are living so far. We went through lots of hardships. We are living under unbearable and unimaginable conditions. However much I try to describe it, I will always fail. But what was life like before this genocide? You know, I can't say that it was like New Zealand. But my heart was light compared to these days, during this genocide. I'm carrying a heaviness, and sometimes I feel like I will collapse because of that heaviness.

Before the genocide I was satisfied that my daughter had both her father and mother, a house, and a room that was special for her. We designed it in a very fantastic and eclectic way for a kid, and, let me say, we had a sense of security. We had access to everything that you need to cope and to live properly, even though the freedom of movement was limited because of the siege and as we don't have an airport here in Gaza. In order to leave, we had to go through Rafah, which is connected to Egypt, then continue by car for a few hours, sometimes days. But we had the option to go and travel and we did so.

On October 2, 2023, Roshdi, Dania, and I travelled to Saudi Arabia and we were planning to go on to Qatar but then the October 7 genocide started, so we cancelled everything and returned to Gaza. I was satisfied in terms of my duties as a mother, and how a mother should provide the baby or kids with all of the means of happiness. The means of a healthy life, a suitable place, a suitable bed, food, and a place to go hike, and all of this stuff.

I feel guilty that we cannot do it now and that I cannot provide my daughter with all of her needs. I somehow feel that I'm failing her because I cannot protect her from the cold and the heat in a tent, and I can't secure her the healthy food that she should be eating. Dania has spent almost four months without getting a single egg, because of the closure of the border and the limitations of the things that come into Gaza. And the same goes for me, chickens and other vegetables and fruits are not available.

Also let me say last, and this is the biggest thing, Dania does not have her father. She lost him when she was eleven months old and I feel that I'm not able to guarantee my life [either], so when it comes to doing [news] coverage, sometimes I take a step back because I don't want to put myself at risk. I don't want to make it worse for her, to lose me as well as her father. I'm not able to be the mother, the father, the son and brother for her. She's our only daughter so I'm trying to be a family for her at the time that she actually doesn't have a family, just me.

Can you tell us about Roshdi, and his work as a journalist and founder of a Palestinian media company, Al-Ain Media?

Roshdi established Al-Ain Media along with his best friend Yaser Murtaja in 2008. Both of them were sharing the same vision, the same mind. They agreed more or less about the Palestinian cause, the valuations that were happening in the occupation, and also about documenting the Israeli crimes in Gaza in particular.

In 2018, the team was documenting the Great March of Return, which was a peaceful march located by the border between Gaza and the occupied territories [the territories occupied by Israel in 1948]. People used to march to demand their rights for return to the occupied lands. The team was documenting this march until an Israeli sniper shot directly at Yaser Murtaja and he died just a few hours after his injury. Five years later, on October 22, 2023, the sixteenth day of the genocide, the Israeli army targeted the family house of Roshdi Sarraj, my husband.

He was a journalist, and when this genocide started we were at the airport. It was the fifth day of our trip [to Saudi Arabia and Qatar]. It was meant to be a two-month trip, but because of the genocide we decided to cancel everything and immediately get back to Gaza. Roshdi believed that he could do something on the ground and that it should be documented and recorded in the media, and that people outside have to know what is happening here. So because he had that sincere feeling of being a journalist, it was his duty to share as much as he could of the Israeli crimes, the Israeli genocide. That's why we decided to get back to Gaza.

Can you describe the day that Roshdi was killed?

The day Roshdi got killed, we were at his family home because our apartment was on a high-level floor [in a tall building], and it was quite dangerous. The family home was a two-storey building with a garden. Roshdi was preparing to get himself ready to do some coverage inside ambulances and I said, 'Roshdi, it's super risky to do this, because since day one they started to hit ambulances.' I freaked out about his safety doing this coverage and then he asked me, 'If I don't do this, who's gonna do it?' So I told him that I totally understood.

We were going to start eating breakfast together, along with his siblings and mother—his father was at his work as he is the municipal mayor of Gaza City [Yahya al-Sarraj]. Then we sat at the table and once we started eating breakfast, we heard a nearby explosion, a very massive one and it turned out to be a carpet bombing, which is several bombings in a row. Actually, this explosion made the table move because of how intense it was. So we ran to the ground floor. When it comes to carpet bombings, it's important to go to the ground floor because of the windows in the above floors but, you know, there is no safe place. If they attack your home, they attack it. It doesn't matter if you are in the above floors or the below ones.

I was holding my Dania, and with my other hand I was holding Roshdi's hand. And then, in two seconds, Roshdi just let go of my hand

and he shielded me. He stood in front of me and gave me a shield [with his body]. At that moment, I was really wondering what he's doing. I just put my hand on his shoulders to say, 'Roshdi, what are you doing?' Then the attack happened.

The Israeli army attacked the home with two rockets from F-16s. In the very beginning, I thought that I lost my [blood sugar] because everything went so grey. I felt dizzy and once you are in the explosion area, you don't hear the explosion because of the pressure. But then I started to smell the gunpowder, the destruction, the burning, the dust, and rubble, and I realised that we had been hit.

I put my hand on my daughter to check her and I found out that she's moving, she's not crying but she's moving. Then I wiped my hand to look for Roshdi and I found nothing. So I turned on the flashlight on my phone and then tried to move. I was unable to move; there was a very heavy thing on my legs. The house was destroyed, collapsed, but nothing had happened to the wall that I was standing on, along with Roshdi's siblings and mother. So I turned on the light and I found that it was Roshdi on my foot, along with lots of concrete and rubble.

I tried to pull his hand and he did not resist. Then the [visibility] started to get a little bit clearer, so his siblings were able to see that he was collapsing. We pulled him out of the rubble and we moved him in front of his house. I touched his face actually to see what his injury was, and he was gasping. He had a one-and-a-half-centimetre crack on his head. It was the trauma of something. His brain was in, not out, but from this crack I could see his brain, the waves of his brain.

I called the ambulances. They said, 'We apologise, we can't come, the entire neighbourhood is being targeted and is under the carpet bombing. Once the carpet bombing is done, we will come.' So I called my brother who is a doctor and I said, 'Hello, we got attacked. Roshdi is suffering from a severe injury ... let me know what I can do.' He said nothing, he just told me to try to go to the hospital on foot.

We put Roshdi on a blanket, and we moved to the hospital on foot. It took us almost fifteen minutes to get to the hospital and the entire area was under intensive attack. Everything was ... I don't know how to describe it. Everything was just flying: the concrete, the stones, the dust, the shrapnel, because they kept on attacking the neighbourhood. We were just moving and there were lots of explosions around us, but we were not terrified, we were just freaked out and numb about what had happened to Roshdi. We just wanted to use every single minute to save his life because he was alive at that time, in his last breaths. We arrived at the hospital and after five to ten minutes, he just passed away.

Do you have any means to process what has happened, to grieve?
Absolutely no. This is not a suitable environment to heal, because we are still under genocide. There is no privacy. We are like five families in one home now, we are almost eighteen people. Like before, when we were in Rafah, in Deir el Belah, it is the same, because we are displaced in groups. You don't have the luxury of breaking down because at such times all you have to do is survive your day, to run for your safety, secure your food, secure the basic needs, and there is not a chance at all to grieve.

And also, somehow, I feel denial because Roshdi's grave is in the north. I am in the south, and I've never actually seen his grave. I think there will be another war after declaring the ceasefire of this war. This war is going to be a lifetime's war that you will never heal from. You will process it in stages, with time, but now, not just me but all Gazans, are stuck in the denial stage because there is no luxury of grief. There is not a suitable time even for psychological therapy, never, because we are still under genocide so it doesn't make sense.

You have continued Roshdi's work stating that 'once you are a journalist, you are a journalist for life'. What does this mean for you and, given the dangers, do you ever consider stopping your work?
Being a journalist for life means that especially under genocide or under occupation, once you choose to become a journalist, it means that you will never have a rest. You will always be on the trigger. There are always lots of things that should be documented.

The Israeli army killed Roshdi, plus almost two hundred other journalists. There are also seventy journalists in jail. The army captured them inside Gaza during the ground invasion. That's why I'm saying that it's a sentence for life, being a journalist, because you cannot stop being a journalist. This genocide has proved that being a journalist puts you on the Israeli list of targets.

I used to be a producer and researcher for Al-Ain Media. I still do that but now my work is more administration related. I have also started making films, so I am a photographer and videographer as well now. I've never thought about stopping my work because I believe that I'm doing something and changing the brainwashed minds outside of Gaza. For example, filming underground and using the English language to address the Western world about the suffering we have endured for fourteen months so far.

If there is anything I can offer, I will do it. It is my duty towards my homeland. All the voices of the people, almost two million in Gaza, trapped, should be heard. Each person has a story and each story is bigger than the other, more worrying. Each story has its own war, its own loss, its own devastation.

When it comes to documenting stories, sometimes you feel like you are hearing from them what you are feeling inside and you are unable to utter the feeling or to articulate it. You cannot be separated from your own grief. Each time it hits you during your work because you are dealing with such devastating stories. These stories always take you back to that zero moment, to that moment that your life changed forever and you go home with a version of the grief of that story, and your own as well. You will touch in each story a different colour of suffering.

This has been the most documented genocide in history, yet it continues. How does that impact how you see your role as a journalist?
It is a televised genocide. It's a livestreamed genocide; we are being slaughtered on the screen with all the faces of killing. We are enduring this killing machine and the world is watching. Sometimes I feel like I've lost my hope in humanity because nobody's able to stop this genocide. Humanity failed us. People show solidarity but solidarity and BDS are not enough. Every single moment there's someone who's killed in a brutal way, so there should be an act to stop this.

But yet, I believe that this televised genocide is televised because of the efforts of the journalists who are all on duty working day and night, not able to sleep, displaced, hungry, terrified, and suffering due to losing dear ones, their homes, their streets ... on duty to continue documenting Israel's crimes.

What are the challenges when reporting? Are there things you are unable to cover?

Absolutely. Being on the scene does not mean what you can just see in the picture. At least at the minimum, you cannot convey the smell of the gunpowder, the dust, the concrete, and the blood. We call this the smell of death. You cannot convey it or transfer it to the audience in a picture or video, never.

We don't have an internet connection because of the attacks on the networks, and this is a challenge in our work. We are also suffering from a lack of equipment, because we got displaced with only one camera. The electricity went off in the second week of the genocide, until now there's no electricity, you cannot just light the room unless you have solar panels, and solar panels actually don't work in winter.

Also there are the problems of transportation. We already lost our car in the bombing, but even if we had the car, we don't have the fuel, so we go on the donkey and some vans and so on that are just running on cooking oil and sometimes cooking gas. This is the crisis of transportation. We [often] walk for hours to arrive at our destination to do our filming. Then there is the issue of getting back and needing the electricity, the internet, to upload the materials. I go to another building now to do the uploading.

The low phone signal is also a challenge, sometimes you arrive in the area to do the filming, then you keep calling the people to film and then, oops, they're not picking up because there is no signal. You went all the way just to arrive and find nobody waiting for you. You're not able to recognise exactly where they are because the strip is already wiped out. There is no remarkable place to direct anybody to, like, 'Hey you can come here, to this place.' No, it's all tents. You will never distinguish any one tent from the thousands of tents around.

And the top priority in all of this is the sense of insecurity, in that you are moving around but not guaranteeing your safety because there are no safe areas, they are just a lie. Thousands have been killed in the 'safe areas'. And for me, sometimes I feel afraid that anything could happen to me during the coverage, and my daughter then loses me and she already lost her father, so this actually freaks me out.

How are journalists in Gaza supporting each other at this time?
We all got displaced without most of our equipment, so we help each other when there is someone in need of a neck mic or a camera, tripod, cable, access to the internet, or to charge batteries. All of this stuff

means nothing to people on the outside but here it means a lot, especially for journalists who got displaced with nothing, actually nothing, like no clothes or belongings. To function properly, you need these supplies or equipment.

Journalists are also supporting each other when someone is coping or dealing with a loss or something. He can ask someone to take charge of his duty for his day and to replace him or her. For journalists, we are not suffering alone. You can share this with your colleagues and it gets listened to when you speak up and when you share how exhausted you are of seeing the coverage and filming the destruction, the calamities, the killed people, the amputees, the injuries. Sometimes it's good to discuss this with someone in the field, someone who can understand you.

Even if there are not any materialistic things you can do for your colleague, there are the spiritual things. You can just support him or her by giving an ear to listen, because sometimes you just feel heavy from what you are seeing every day. You need to speak about it and share it with your colleagues, and they can support you and you will not be alone. And sometimes when you are just sharing silence with them, it also means a lot.

You recently received the 2024 International Press Freedom Award. Have you felt supported by international media organisations and journalists? If not, what should they be doing?
Yes, receiving the award showed me that there are people who care. There are people outside who are interested in the Palestinian cause and believe in our abilities, in documenting and filming under inhuman and terrifying circumstances.

It is a good sign, especially at the moment with everything. It's a boost that my work, my coverage, is being recorded and awarded and people know how tired we are and they are showing support. So yes, it shows that the award is an act of, 'Hello, we are here, we hear you, we feel you.'

What are your hopes for your daughter and for Gaza / your homeland?
My hope for my daughter, for Gaza, and my homeland is something that I hope too. That we will live in that era, that period, when Palestine would be free, *khalas* [enough]. We're done with the bloodshed, the

massacres, it's time to be free, to be liberated from the occupation. So my hope for my daughter, my Gaza, is to live with peace without occupation and to free Palestine. Once Palestine is free, the trauma stops, the suffering, the siege, that history of suffering, all of that is going to stop with this.

Rana Abu Rahmah

Rana is from Nablus, West Bank. She currently lives in Bil'in village, West Bank. She is a journalist and filmmaker who has been involved in the popular struggle against the Israeli occupation. We interviewed Rana in August 2018 at her home in Bil'in. As we spoke, her family were watching live footage of the Great March for Return protests in Gaza.

Could you tell us a bit about your background?
I moved to Bil'in when I married my husband Ashraf. I'm originally from Nablus, and I used to live in a camp called Camp Number One, because it was the first camp established [in Nablus].[1] I first became an activist, and then a journalist. But I didn't study journalism—I studied business management.

After I finished high school, I worked on a local TV channel called Al-Afaq—which means 'horizons'—but it was shut down by the Israeli army in 2015. At Al-Afaq we covered breaking news and we followed everything up 24/7, so the army felt that this threatened them and their plans. They came and invaded the building, which was in Area A [the area of the West Bank designated as under Palestinian control] and sealed it off.

1 According to the United Nations Reliefs Works Agency (UNWRA): 'Camp No. 1 was established in 1950 and borders the Nablus municipality. It was the first camp established in the Nablus area and was thus named Camp No. 1. It is also known as Ein Beit el-Ma'. Israeli army incursions into the camp are not uncommon and frequently result in arrests, as well as damage to homes.' With nearly 9,700 registered persons in the camp, Camp No. 1 is the West Bank's most densely populated camp.

I was also in a campaign called We Refuse to Die Silently, based in a few places in the West Bank. I was the only woman in the campaign, except for Nariman Tamimi [a woman involved in the popular resistance from the village of Nabi Saleh]. We would have four people in a car—a driver, a Palestinian volunteer, an international volunteer, and a Palestinian journalist—and go to the villages located close to settlements to help people gather olives from their farms [Palestinian farmers are routinely harassed by the settlers and army when picking their olives]. The camera can somehow protect people from the soldiers. We documented a lot of things that the soldiers and the settlers did. The international volunteers were from ISM [International Solidarity Movement].

Were you treated with respect by the men in the campaign?
No, it wasn't easy. The men had this thing about thinking they were stronger, even though I did the same job as them. When settlers or soldiers came, the men would say to be careful and try to keep me back. But during those moments I didn't think about if I was a man or a woman: I was just thinking that something should be done.

Every Friday we used to go to [the village of] Kufr Qadum—which is close to Nablus—to be with the local people and film the protests. On the first anniversary of the Kufr Qadum protests, I made a film about the village and gave it to the people. I kept on going there for about two years.

How did the men react to you in Kufr Qadum?
When I first went there, they asked me why I was there. 'There are enough people here', they said, 'so why a woman?' Sometimes I felt that this view existed in how people looked at me, even if they didn't say anything. My counter-argument whenever we had this discussion was: 'I'm standing next to an international woman [activist] and I'm doing exactly what she does, so why should I stay at home?' Then we started to ask, why don't the women of the village participate? So we became involved in talking with women. For example, I saw an old woman who was participating in activities resisting the occupation running after a soldier with her shoe.

There was no filming at first in Kufr Qadum, I was the first one to do it. So this established my reputation there. I proposed establishing a media unit. I went and started training [people in media], and I became a trainer for the people who went into the field. Since then, a lot of barriers vanished. So it was difficult but not impossible.

Were you scared, being in Kufr Qadum while soldiers were firing at demonstrators?

It's dangerous in Kufr Qadum because there's one street, and on either side is olive groves and there is a big risk that you will either get shot or arrested. Of course I was scared. I was once hit by a tear gas bomb. I didn't go to the hospital, but it has affected my back.

Can you tell us about your work supporting the families of prisoners?

There was a man called Khader Adnan who was on hunger strike in prison for about two months.[2] Because of that I became more involved in working with the families of prisoners. We used to put up protest tents so the families of prisoners would gather there. We filmed the protests and other activities and I made a film about it, along with a director. The protests were mainly in city centres like Arafat Square in Ramallah, and sometimes at other places like Ofer prison [a military prison close to Ramallah]. A lot of prisoners' families used to go there.

We started the Asra Voice—Voice of the Prisoners—radio network, and I worked on it from 2012 to 2015. The prisoners' families called the radio station and talked about their sons. The prisoners could also hear the radio in jail. It was a connection between the families of the prisoners and the prisoners themselves. I was one of the people responsible for preparing the day-to-day tasks of the show, and I used to interview the families at the protest tents. I'd also go to the prisoners' families' houses and record what they said for the radio show. We used to choose the families who had special cases: for example, those whose parents were very old and couldn't visit their son, or those who were not allowed to visit their relatives in jail.

There was a programme for prisoners and a programme for families of martyrs [people who have lost their lives as a result of Israel's occupation]. I started as a volunteer and then they gave me basic expenses to work on the other show about the martyrs.

---

2 Khader Adnan went on hunger strike for sixty-six days in 2012, bringing him close to death. He was released as a result of the hunger strike, but has subsequently been arrested several times.

How do you think the presence of cameras at a demonstration changes things?

The presence of cameras is very important. A good example is when my husband Ashraf's own phone was used to film his arrest. To give another example, Ashraf's brother Bassem was [fatally] shot in 2009.[3] The camera was there but the ambulance was not. His sister Jawaher inhaled tear gas mixed with white phosphorus but when she died, there was no camera.[4]

Rana's husband Ashraf interrupts to explain what happened to his brother: Bassem was asking the soldiers not to shoot tear gas because there were sheep in the area. So they shot him with a [high velocity] tear gas canister straight into his heart. This canister can travel a kilometre and a half in distance, and the way the soldiers used it is illegal. The soldiers were close to Bassem and the canister opened his chest and went in by about ten centimetres.

Rana continues: The camera showed the reality of what happened to Bassem. The soldiers said that the canister ricocheted off a post and then into his chest. But the video showed exactly what happened. If there's no camera, the occupation will always refute what actually happened. These videos show the reality of what actually happens.

---

3 According to the Forensic Architecture website:

> On 17 April 2009, near the village of Bil'in, Bassem Abu Rahma was shot and killed by a tear-gas canister fired across the fence of the barrier wall that surrounds the West Bank. Abu Rahma was attending a protest, and was unarmed.
>
> The protest occurred at a location that had been declared a 'closed military zone' by Israeli authorities four years earlier. Since then, non-violent activists were routinely arrested and imprisoned in the area.
>
> In the context of such encounters, official instructions allow soldiers to use only 'non-lethal means', such as tear gas and rubber-coated bullets, unless their lives are in danger. But while tear gas is considered a 'non-lethal' munition, when the aluminum gas canister hits a human body directly, the impact can be fatal. Soldiers are only supposed to shoot these munitions upward, at a trajectory of 60 degrees, above a crowd.

Following Abu Rahma's death, the military denied responsibility, claiming that soldiers did not fire the canister directly at the victim.

4 An Independent Middle East Media Center news report from January 2011 reads:

> Jawaher Abu Rahma, aged 35, died on Saturday, after suffering the effects of tear gas inhalation fired by the Israeli military during the Friday weekly protest in Bil'in. Medical sources reported that the cause of the death was suffocation from tear gas chemicals mixed with phosphorus. Hundreds of Palestinians, internationals and Israeli peace activists attended Abu Rahma's funeral in a procession through the village of Bil'in on Saturday, in which residents released a statement condemning the death.

The Israeli army tries to delete videos like this. All of a sudden you see that videos like this disappear.

In October 2017 the soldiers raided our house at 3.00am, along with other families in the village. They wanted to talk to Ashraf, but Ashraf wasn't there. I filmed when they came in. My voice was loud because I was stressed. The soldiers told me not to speak. In the video I was saying 'Don't touch anything'. They were checking everything, and I was filming them. They took all of our devices and technology. During the raid, the soldiers had a scary-looking person with them, who had his face covered and wore gloves. He looked like a technology expert. They must have had something that tracks technology because they went straight to our closet and found a hard disk.

We had lost any hope of getting our devices back, but they returned them after two months. When we got them back, they were broken. They hacked the phone so whatever SIM card you put in, it doesn't work anymore.

The Israeli authorities are trying to make it illegal for people to film the army.[5] What do you think of that?

They don't want their crimes to be documented. This proposed law means that whoever takes photos or videos of soldiers will go to jail for five to ten years. But if we stick to every new law imposed by the occupation, we won't be able to leave our houses. We are under occupation and there is no justice under occupation. People won't care about this new law: they will keep filming. Their videos are holy to them—for example, when they want to show evidence in court of people throwing rocks—but filming is a crime for us.

They came up with this law because Imad Abu Shamsiyah filmed the murder of a young man, shot [by an Israeli soldier] in Hebron. So nowadays the cameras scare them. They have recently shot journalists [for example on the Great March of Return protests in Gaza].[6] If they don't shoot them, they arrest them. The camera is the first line of defence.

---

5 In 2018 a bill titled the 'Prohibition Against Photographing and Documenting IDF Soldiers' was presented to the Israeli parliament. The bill aimed to make the photographing of soldiers punishable by ten years in prison.

6 For example, soldiers shot and killed Yaser Murtaja during the Great March of Return protests. He was wearing a jacket emblazoned with the word 'Press'.

In Gaza, on the Great March of Return, they have been targeting journalists . . .

They are targeting the elements that are saving people's lives. Of course they target journalists, especially since Palestine became a member of the UN. Israel felt that the PA would somehow sue them under international law using the evidence gathered by journalists. Now Palestine will sue Israel under international law because of [evidence provided by] the cameras—we have the evidence and the Palestinian narrative is winning over the Israeli one.

Are you still doing videography?

After moving to Bil'in I stopped doing video journalism. There are a lot of journalists in Bil'in and it's a small village!

Are there any organisations for female journalists in Palestine?

No. There are no possibilities for such a thing. Equipment is also a problem. I have been to a lot of demonstrations but I'm never wearing a bulletproof vest. I don't have one because they're very expensive and there's no one to give it to me.

Do you think it is more difficult for a woman to get involved in political organising in the West Bank than it is for a man?

Yes, it's not easy, because our society is conservative. In terms of filming, I felt that the camera gave me strength. It felt like a person supporting me. And when I became involved with the prisoners and their families, I acted out of empathy because one day I might be the one who needs support when someone I love goes to jail.

Shatha Abu Srour

Shatha is from Aida refugee camp in Bethlehem, West Bank. She currently lives in Beit Jala, Bethlehem. Shatha is a disability activist and coordinator of the Palestinian Disability Coalition. She and others carried out a sixty-three-day sit-in at the Palestinian Legislative Council building in 2021. She is blind, among other characteristics. We interviewed Shatha in February 2025, via two phone calls.

Can you tell us about where you grew up and where you consider home to be?

I was born in Aida refugee camp in Bethlehem. There are many refugee Palestinians who moved to the camp in 1948, and then again in 1967. This is where my grandfather happened to move to, he was originally from a village within the Green Line called Beit Nattif [near Jerusalem]. It is not easy for someone who was born in a refugee camp to answer the question, 'Where do you live?' Usually we come with this story: we were born in the camp but it's not our original place. Our family later moved from Aida to an area in Bethlehem called Beit Jala.

My grandfather didn't want to move from the camp because he always had this dream that he would return back to his village where he had a lot of land. There was no need, in his opinion, to buy land in Bethlehem. My grandmother had a different idea—she decided that no, we want to live around here [in Beit Jala] to make it easier for us to have more space. So she went against my grandfather's desire and bought this land. Almost all of her sons are using this land, and her granddaughters and grandsons as well.

When I was young the camp was not the friendliest place to be in when it comes to my experience with disability. I remember when I was maybe three or four years old, I'd be dealing with some bullying in the street when I would impose myself on other children. They would be playing with something and I would put myself in the middle of whatever they were playing and then they would kick me away. I would go crying to my mother.

I think I was three and a half when a director of a boarding school visited us at home and told my mother about the school and that it was my only chance to access education. It wasn't easy for my mother at first but they started telling her that 'if you refuse, you have to consider that maybe it's selfish to be thinking only about yourself; you have to consider your daughter's future', eventually she decided to go ahead.

At first, we would visit our families every week or every other week, but then after the Oslo Accords, many checkpoints were established between the cities. The school was in Jerusalem and we lived in Bethlehem, so checkpoints made it harder for us to make those journeys home. Sometimes it would take one or two months until we had a chance to visit our families.

Home is not a place necessarily, it is rather an idea, a feeling, or certain people.

Were you born with a visual impairment?

Yes, and I would say that as a child you think that all of you are the same, right? I wanted to play, just like my siblings or cousins, to go to the garden, to do this and that. I would be surprised when there would be things they would do that I wouldn't. For example, when I would fall over a stone, or from a tree, and they wouldn't.

The way I think of it is that nobody came to tell me 'Hey Shatha, you are blind and this is what it means.' The reason why I say that is because I have a younger sister who is also blind. When she was young, maybe four or five years old, I heard her asking my mother, 'Do you see?' My mum would say yes. 'Does this person see?' She'd say yes. Then my sister would ask, 'Do I see?' I didn't have a chance for someone to explain this to me, in order for me to have been able to tell my sister.

If I hadn't had my parents always trying to do something about me being blind, I would have always been content. Really. But they always kept trying this doctor, that doctor. I was in my twelfth grade and this was the last chance for my mother. We visited a doctor and I remember him telling her: 'The way you are doing it is making it hard for your daughter to adapt. Until now, medicine didn't find a solution for this exact issue she has … you need to accept her for who she is.' I was so grateful for him because I didn't know how to say the same thing to my mother: 'You're making it harder for me.' She thought that she was doing her job and I understand that. She didn't want to feel that there was something she could have done and didn't.

When you are younger, you don't think of it in this way. I was angry with her because she kept wanting me to see. I kept telling her, 'I'm happy as I am.' More than that, I felt like being blind made it easier for me to do things that people my age couldn't. For example, going out with a friend and staying as long as I wanted. I remember the first fight with my mother was when I came back really late and my mum was saying, 'What will people say?' I said, 'People usually don't notice me, why would they see me coming late?' I wasn't scared, and I never fought with this part of me. It felt like it gave me a green light to be and do what I want.

What was it like growing up with a disability in Palestine, how inclusive was it? Has there been a change since then regarding rights for people with disabilities?

Yes, but it's still hard. I think there would be less bullying now, regarding my own experience, but it doesn't mean that other people don't experience that [bullying]. I think it comes down to the type of disability now unfortunately.

Many groups in Palestine, including those with disabilities, don't necessarily feel welcome, which affects our enjoyment of rights and access to services. It also affects our social participation, and to some of us, our sense of belonging. If I didn't have a duty to stay in Palestine—as our struggle is existential—maybe I would explore other places, where I can be myself. This is not only about my experience with disability, but about other parts of me.

I grew up during the First Intifada in Palestine. This Intifada resulted in an increased number of people with disabilities, of course. It's a policy of the coloniser. Many of those who were injured and acquired a permanent disability were seen or perceived as fighters by their peers, as people who sacrificed for the Palestinian cause. So I think that impacted on how Palestinian society started perceiving disability. Although I would say that people who acquired a permanent disability in this way don't see themselves as having a disability. Like they wouldn't be with us in battles, they have their own battles when it comes to fighting for better rights or services. I hate to say 'theirs' and 'ours', but that's what it is so far.

So were people that acquired a disability in the First Intifada considered as having a higher status as a result of fighting, whether or not they fought?

Yes, but it gave people with disabilities a chance to be noticed. This is what I heard people with disabilities who were activists in this era say as well. In the beginning, it had a positive impact on rehabilitative services. Many people who were injured or who had disabilities since birth noticed that rehabilitation services were better and more affordable during Yassar Arafat's term [as president of the Palestinian Authority, between 1994 and 2004].

This was up until the end of the Second Intifada [January 1, 2005], and up until Abu Mazen started his presidency [January 15, 2005]. Abu Mazen has his own opinion; he doesn't necessarily encourage resistance as a choice and so he also wouldn't think of rehabilitation as a priority.

You co-organised a sixty-three-day sit-in outside the offices of the Palestinian Legislative Council (PLC) in Ramallah in 2021, demanding the right to comprehensive health insurance for people with disabilities. This right had been stipulated in Palestinian basic law but not acted upon.[1] Can you tell us about it?

It wasn't our first attempt, meaning it wasn't our first step. I, and other people, had been involved in many other advocacy campaigns since 2012, and some of us started earlier when it came to health rights. I can name many attempts that we tried before the sit-in, and, unfortunately, they were not successful. The Ministry of Health was the most arrogant ministry when it came to rights for people with disabilities. They were less receptive. And so we had to do the sit-in.

---

1 The Palestinian Basic Law was designed to function as a temporary constitution for the Palestinian Authority, until the establishment of an independent state and a permanent constitution for Palestine was to be achieved. The Basic Law was passed by the Palestinian Legislative Council in 1997 and ratified by President Yasser Arafat in 2002. See https://www.palestinianbasiclaw.org.

We were not affiliated to any entity, we were just a group of people, even though some of us were employees in this or that organisation. When we decided we wanted to do the sit-in, we took days off for it. We were the ones to decide when we wanted to start and when we wanted to go home, what would have made us do this and what would have made us do that. We didn't want anyone to influence our decisions. This made it hard for the Palestinian Authority (PA). It's easier when political parties, trade unions, or organisations are doing this. The PA can influence them and have something to threaten them with—their bank accounts, for example. But there was nothing they could have done to stop us, but to comply. Especially because our demand was already in Palestinian Basic Law, since 2003.

If we had a state of Palestine for real, it would be stated that inclusive health insurance is the right of people with disabilities. Any law should be in line with the Basic Law, otherwise there is a constitutional imbalance. So legally speaking there was nothing the PA could do to argue against our demands. Also, they had nothing against us as people and, even if they did, they knew that to argue with us would not have been successful.

What made it even harder for the PA was the fact that many groups of people with disabilities started supporting our demands. They came from different cities and protested outside the Palestinian Authority Legislative Council building [also known as the Palestinian Parliament], in support of our demands for health insurance. And slowly other entities started supporting us, including activists from different groups—women or people who were interested in social justice, human rights activists, journalists, and other coalitions, including the Palestinian Disability Coalition, which was with us from almost the second day.

It was strange, the PA didn't know what to do with us. It was the first time that a group—whether with disabilities or not—had occupied a governmental building. We learnt it from other movements in the world. Actually, it was our second time, the first time we also did it, in 2018, also in the Legislative Council Building—it's accessible—and symbolically, it's the voice of the people.

In 2018, our fight was against the Palestine Liberation Organisation (PLO), because we wanted the Palestinian General Union of Persons with Disabilities (GUPD) to be represented within the organisation.

This union was established in the early 1990s and was promised membership in the PLO, just like other unions, but it didn't happen. Then other things happened: between 2010 and 2018, no political elections were taking place; many offices were not accessible; there was no representation for persons with a learning disability; and no full and effective membership in the PLO. We tried to work with our colleagues in order to solve those problems, no success. Thus, we tried the sit-in.

We learnt something very interesting. In our fight with the PLO, we stayed in the Legislative Council building for four days. In our fight for health insurance, we stayed for sixty-three and a half days. In these four days, we saw many people, and way more politicians than those we met in the sixty-three days. This was because the fight was different, it was purely political.

If you don't have the means or the willingness to play dirty games, you will not succeed. Political battles require tools that we don't have, and we don't want to have. It's okay, we failed in this one. We learnt about the accusations they held against us, and also how to manage negotiations, focus on the goal, deal with conflicts, and build a strong group. We just wanted representation, but how it was to be manifested was not worth it. Any fight that has to do with organisations is not worth it.[2]

How did you manage the sixty-three-day sit-in practically? And what was the outcome?

We stayed day and night. There were only five of us inside. From the second day, other people started coming, but the only people that would stay day and night in the Legislative Council were us. It was during COVID and we didn't want them [the PA officials] to tell us, 'There's a crowd, there's too many people, you can't do this, you have to go home.' We didn't want to give them this excuse. We were there for a long time. It will always be a shame on them, that it took sixty-three days to achieve our rights that were already included in the Basic Law, it wasn't like we were demanding a new law.

---

2 The GUPD remains as an independent and supervisory body outside of the PLO. It works in parallel with the Independent Commission for Human Rights to incorporate policies and regulations within Palestine's Basic Law. See https://www.ohchr.org/en/treaty-bodies/crpd/state-palestine-imm-situation.

What made it easier in some way was the fact that when we were three or four days in, we started working with one of our friends who is an expert in drafting laws and by-laws. We began writing a draft by-law that responded to our demands, and this made for a shift. We were not only telling the PA about the problem, but presenting the solution and fighting for it. I think this was a great move from the movement side. Instead of telling the PA that there was this problem and that problem when it came to our health rights—like family members not being included, health services not being free, and maybe not available, etc.—we designed the solution, which was the by-law. That started being our advocacy tool and it made it easier for negotiations afterwards.

On the forty-third day, I think, we met with the prime minister and one of the things we demanded was the draft [by-law] we designed to be the basis of our negotiations. The prime minister gave orders in this regard because the Ministry of Health wouldn't have accepted it otherwise. Even so, at first the prime minister and Ministry of Health [offered token gestures] instead of accepting the by-law. They said, 'If you don't want to pay the 5 or 10 percent towards health insurance, then okay, we don't want it. If you want assistant devices, just come to us and we'll work it out.' And things like that. Then we had to come back with the human rights discourse; that we were talking about human rights, not charity cases.

The by-law was eventually accepted after sixty-three days, which is how and why we ended the sit-in. However, in our last press conference, we made it clear that this was the first step, and that it was everybody's responsibility to use it as an advocacy tool, fighting for its implementation. We had afterwards some small battles regarding the implementation, all the way until the war [on Gaza] started.

There was little English-language media coverage of the sit-in, was there more coverage in Arabic-language media? And do you think disability struggles in Palestine are given the attention they deserve?
I can't make judgements; I can just tell you what happened with us. When we were at the sit-in, someone who wasn't Palestinian said, 'If we belonged to an organisation or entity, I could make your story go all over the place.' The fact that we were just a group of people wasn't intriguing. She kept telling us this and we said, 'Okay, we don't want

this coverage, easy. We want the by-law. They give us the by-law, we go home.'

I would say there was [more Arabic language coverage]. There were radio stations who would call us at least once a week. Of course, national Palestine TV did not, because they had to say what the government wanted them to say, but other media agencies did, including ones that cover the region. Al Jazeera was interested and there was an article written by *Middle East Eye*. But they took what they wanted and cut what they didn't want, because the way we have built our discourse doesn't attract many people.

We don't separate our activism regarding disability from our activism in wanting Palestine to be free. We always think that there are so many ways to resist and one of them is to have a society of fighters. We don't say yes to everything, when it's against our rights and dignity, we learn to say no. And if we learn how to say no, then slowly it will find its way against the occupation as well.

The other thing I have in my mind is, how can we expect people who don't have their basic rights met to reject the occupation and find their ways of rejecting the occupation. Maybe they reject it but they don't know how to do it. If you are hungry and there isn't this collective movement in your society for hungry people, each person will be waiting for the other to do something. But once you do this in terms of advocacy campaigns and are successful, then something will accumulate in the consciousness of society members—[the feeling that] it can be done.

You mentioned that you don't separate your activism for disability rights from your activism in wanting Palestine to be free, could you explain a bit more about this?

I think that this has to do with several things, some of them are maybe individual, some of them have a nationalistic nature. The individual or personal part has to do with being born in a refugee camp. I lived this experience when I was a child, checkpoints hindered connections with my family.

Also, a major thing for me has been that one of my closest relatives, my uncle, has been in prison for thirty-three years. During this time, we have kept communicating by whatever means available. He's my spiritual, intellectual companion. He's very close to me, not only because he's my uncle, but we have this companionship in life where we have supported each other in so many ways, even though our communication method has changed according to the circumstances. I can't speak about my life and about how we make connections without coming to this friendship.

In our activism on disability, colleagues, friends, and I have noticed this big connection between colonial policies and practices and disablement. Maybe equally important is the fact that we are under occupation, with or without disabilities, and we know this the day that we know we are Palestinian. Sometimes being Palestinian comes first and foremost, up and above any other identifying characteristic, and so as activists we always make efforts to contribute in drawing the lines between all intersections: disability, activism, liberation, change, colonization, etc. I have always sought to be involved with groups that recognise this fact, that being Palestinian comes above everything.

We have duties here, so any time there is something happening, it's a must that we have to be in it and on it and we have a word to say, not only when it comes to disability, but about Palestine and violations carried out by the Israeli occupation. If there is a connection between the occupation and disability, there is, and if there isn't, there isn't. For example, when this genocidal war started in Gaza, other groups started reaching out to us. It was important for coalitions to take positions, explore how to contribute to challenging the Israeli narrative, and consider how to represent our people who didn't have the luxury of representing themselves. I'm saying this as an example of how people see us and other groups, and whether they will approach us or not. It's known by other groups that we don't only do disability-specific things, but we also have something to say when it comes to other national issues.

Are you connected with disability activists in Gaza, or people living with disabilities in Gaza?

Of course, yes. For example, now I am coordinating Palestinian Disability Coalition work and the coalition has members from Gaza as well. This is important because we want to fight whatever is happening geographically and demographically. It's one of our principles to make sure we have members from Gaza and we reflect it in our rules as a coalition. One hand alone cannot clap, as they say. I also have friends in Gaza and we always keep in touch. The reason why I mention the coalition here is because I believe deeply in collective efforts.

Have your colleagues and friends in Gaza asked for particular support, with the increase in people living with disability as a result of the genocide?

First, it was important for them that we keep in touch and that we do whatever was necessary for monitoring and amplifying their voices. And then, of course, they have been asking for certain kinds of initiatives, for example, specific camps for Palestinians with disabilities because they have less access to humanitarian aid, they are more vulnerable. I don't like to use this word but they had less chances, even before the war, to be included in the economic sector and so on. Anyone who is interested in this issue knows that there are huge gaps between what one wishes they could do and what the situation is for people with disabilities in Gaza. We couldn't set up specific camps because they would have been targeted. People had many question marks regarding what was safe and where it was safe. You know, no place in Gaza was safe.

I believe each person who cares has been able to find one way or another to support. But from my experience, I can say that people with disabilities, as well as other Palestinians, have been needing to feel that they are not alone, have needed the practical means to support their choice to stay in Gaza, to be included equitably in humanitarian interventions, and to have their right to inherent dignity and self-determination supported.

We tried to influence UN special rapporteurs, for example, Francesca Albanese, the special rapporteur on the situation of human rights in the occupied Palestinian territories and Dr. Heba Hagrass, the special rapporteur on the rights of persons with disabilities. They were also able to influence other special rapporteurs, so we met with them several times. They made releases and wrote a letter to the Israeli government, etc. But I have to admit, we lost belief in the international human rights machinery. We were going for such attempts because our colleagues and friends in Gaza always said, 'We need to keep trying, we must not leave any door, any platform, any person who may push for a good change.'

We also made connections with other activists with disabilities outside Palestine who have been willing to take action. This was important because this war was very intensive and we, as activists, were in shock. We didn't know what to do and how to do it and how to be influential—how to do something that really mattered. We trivialised so many things because we felt like they didn't speak to people on the ground, but then slowly we recognised that we can do what we can do. Those friends or colleagues who started communicating with us from other areas in the world made it more possible to do what we did. It felt better than doing nothing.

Have you worked with Palestinians with disabilities in prisons?
Up until now prisons have been going through an unprecedented era in some way. Prisons became like small Gazas. Everything was happening inside them but with less coverage than Gaza.

Whoever is following this issue will notice the difference between people who were in prisons already at the beginning of the war and who were then released during this time. They [Israeli prison staff] took all of their belongings, clothes, blankets, mattresses. There has been violence in all of its forms: physical, sexual, psychological. There has been isolation—family visits stopped until now—only lawyers have been able to make irregular visits. This has affected me personally too. I have had to use many tactics to deal with it, it hasn't been easy.

I have to say that Palestinian prisoners present a deep wound in the Palestinian conscience. Many of them have life sentences, many actually have six and nine life sentences. We used to learn that the liberation movements, as well as daughters and sons of the revolutions, should not leave their people in prison. I personally live the life sentence but from the other side of it. This and more made it important for me to explore how to address Palestinian political prisoners with disability.

Together with other friends and colleagues I started to monitor the response to the Israeli report on the UN Convention on the Rights of Persons with Disabilities in 2020. I noticed the poor legal assistance some people with disabilities experience. Many acquire disability as a result of torturous Israeli policies and practices [in prison]. They then struggle to access medical services once they are released. Finally, we started thinking of how to systemically work on this issue with the relevant formal entities. But, unfortunately, we are at a time where, in my opinion, anyone who thinks that systemic change is possible under the PA does not read the situation clearly.

How can solidarity activists around the world, with disabilities and without, support people with disabilities in Gaza, the West Bank, and beyond?

This is a very hard question because those of us living it don't know what is possible, and this is a question I would ask to my friends in Gaza, 'What can we do?' They would say something like, 'We are really in a state of freeze, we don't know what to think, we don't know.' I thought that asking people would help me know what to do and then I discovered that no, they are really in a place where they need someone to think on their behalf, and sometimes I've experienced the same thing. It's not always possible for us to answer this question, but what matters at the end of the day is to know that you are not alone, in whatever way other people can make this possible, and it matters a lot.

This world is not made for justice, let's face it and be honest at least with ourselves. There are places where human beings carry good values, in the simplest ways that exist, it doesn't have to be complicated.

Do you feel that you experience triple oppression—as a woman, as a Palestinian living under occupation, and as a person with a disability?

I will say something that I really feel and live and experience, so it's not like a slogan. I believe—and it cannot be generalised, that people live with different characteristics. In this life they will be given different opportunities, which makes for some beliefs, and beliefs become practices, and practices become lifestyles, and these translate themselves into choices.

The way I think of oppression is that it's something that can be an idea that people can fight in themselves. Yes, there is oppression, yes there are violations to human rights and to humanity in general here in Palestine, but what will I benefit by calling myself oppressed or a victim? How will it be useful for me as someone who is looking for ways to change? It won't because if I get lost in this description or category, I will just learn to receive or take, or learn to wait, or learn to cry.

So the way I think of it is how to convert or try to convert oppression, rage, anger, frustration, into something that is useful for me and my people. Sometimes I succeed, sometimes I fail. You don't have to succeed all the time, and I don't succeed all the time, of course. I don't like thoughts and ideas that perpetuate helplessness, this is what I'm trying to say.

Do you think the movement for disability justice is growing in Palestine?

No, I don't think so. It's in a state of unknown I would say, in a state of re-identification, just like so many things. Even people who are really connected, and mean to be connected to each and every thing that is happening is in the midst of re-identification. Nobody who cares can be the same as they were before this genocidal war and everything that came with it.

But in many ways the same thing that happened in Gaza is now happening in the north [of the West Bank], with less coverage. The world knows less about it. For example, Al Jazeera has been suspended from reporting by Israel and by the Palestinian Authority. In August, on air, an Israeli soldier came up to Al Jazeera presenters and asked them to stop broadcasting. The same thing happened, on air, with a Palestinian security agent who gave staff a letter and asked them to stop.

It's interesting because the PA is also doing this in many ways to Palestinians in the north. They are trying to do things that the Israelis do. When the PA arrests people, they use the same methods, as if they are trained together, or as if there is something they want to do with our heads. The same thing will happen in Ramallah, in Bethlehem, in Hebron, in every city where people are living. It's a matter of time, you know. We will be living the same thing that Gaza lived, but with less coverage.

Back to the movement, when military attacks increased in Gaza, it changed our priorities, and meant that we couldn't work on advocacy the same way that we were working on it before. It's hard to campaign for access to health rights when the whole region, not just the country, is on the edge of hell. This doesn't make sense; it's not relevant. Even though one would think, well, how can we be resilient if people are sick or people need health services or if people are homeless? Still, we do what we can in terms of access to services, but we can't do it in the same way we would do advocacy before. We would not gain solidarity and support from other movements or people. It's not easy.

We continue to do monitoring. I try to be involved in different research, at least to contribute to knowledge production so people have the chance to share their experiences in the way they want.

What about advocacy organisations in the West Bank?

As I mentioned, rehabilitation services were better [under Arafat], but also once the UN Convention on the Rights of Persons with Disabilities (CRPD) came into force [between 2006 and 2008], many donors in Palestine started pushing NGOs to change a lot of their work. Organisations moved from service design and provision to advocacy based on the convention. Advocacy without being necessarily localised or contextualised. The shift happened in the discourse but they didn't take the time for it to be real, for it to be natural, which is why we didn't necessarily notice it in other areas apart from policies and practices. Immediately after that, we started noticing donors influencing NGOs; they wanted training based on, and advocacy campaigns to be based on, the convention. This was even before Palestine acceded to the Convention on the Rights of Persons with Disabilities.

Is there anything else you would like to say?

Nothing can be done by one person. One person can maybe make an influence here and there, connect the dots, but cannot do much alone. It's people together that make for powerful impacts. And what we realised, as the movement that did the sit-in, was that the more we say things, the more people live them, the more you're connected with people.

For example, almost every day during the sit-in, we would inform people of what happened, have openness to other ideas, and the capacity to apologise when we made mistakes. All those things we learnt with and from people. Nobody can claim that they are anything but what others influence within them.

Ghada Hamdan

Ghada Hamdan (a pseudonym) is from Bil'in. She currently lives on Om Sleiman, a permaculture farm established in the village of Bil'in in the West Bank. The farm is situated on a piece of land that has been the subject of years of struggle. It lies close to the Israeli colony of Modi'in Illit, in 'Area C', meaning that the land is under full Israeli control. Palestinian farmers of Om Sleiman are forbidden from building any structures, including wells. We interviewed Ghada in July 2018 in Nablus.

Can you tell us about why you chose to be involved in land-based organising?
I choose farming as a form of activism and resistance, especially agroecology because it gives you tools to have control over your resources and to be independent and self-reliant. I'm really interested in self-sufficiency because that's what we really need in Palestine. Palestinians are occupied and thus our resources are occupied. Over the years our electricity, water, and food has come from our occupier, Israel. Israel controls everything; we don't even have an independent economy of our own and this creates a population who are unable to achieve independence. We have to learn to be independent, self-sufficient, to harvest our own water, grow our crops, and save our seeds.

There was a big movement aimed at building self-sufficiency and autonomy during the First Intifada. Has the situation changed now?
The structures of our neighbourhoods in the First Intifada were different. Back then people lived in small organised communities and everyone knew each other and wanted to support each other and

would know what each community member could offer. You had the farmer, the cheese maker, the people who did maintenance, the teacher, the healer. People needed each other.

Now the sense of community and voluntary work has changed due to the difficult circumstances Palestinians live under. People are more concerned with their own personal needs and now in the cities people don't necessarily know who their neighbour is. This is especially the case in Ramallah and in Jerusalem. The young generation is moving away from the villages where agricultural land is, looking for better opportunities. Nevertheless we are seeing collectives and movements who are working towards building resilient communities and supporting each other when needed. For example, more farmers' markets have started to support farmers to sell their products, and consumers are more aware about the origin of the products they buy.

Are co-operatives politically significant for you?
Definitely. I think that any groups who share similar needs or objectives can come together and have stronger influence and share the risk and financial burden of starting a project, as well as provide emotional support to each other in times of need. But it has to be done very carefully. I have seen many co-operatives fall apart because of social clashes or personal interest, or because of the lack of self-organisation. The villages used to be a good [co-operative] system; for example, a villager would have a field of corn and people would help and share the food. There was a more voluntary way of living. Now we have moved a bit from these terms and way of living together.

How strong are ecological movements in Palestine?
'Ecological movement' as a term doesn't really exist. I would say people are more aware of the environment and ecology, but to be honest it is also a privilege here to be concerned with ecology. Ecological farms and agroecology nevertheless are growing stronger and that is not related to privilege. Palestine has historically been a fertile land with peasants growing food for their own households, so it is not something new to us and not a trend. Taking in consideration the lack of support, especially financially, for new co-operative projects, and the challenges that come with starting movements or start-ups in an occupied place, I would say that there is a strong movement, especially in small-scale farming.

The system has created a comfortable bubble. It's created a situation where it's difficult to imagine an alternative way of living. It's a system that makes you want to stay inside it, even if you hate it. You are in the office 8.00am till 4.00pm, and go out at the weekend, and repeat. One of the hardest things is to get out of your comfort zone and head towards an alternative way of life. If you're producing your own food, that's already an alternative. If you quit your job, that's an alternative. If you make your own vinegar, oil, or cheese, that's an alternative. If you build your house from mud [a traditional Palestinian building style], that's an alternative.

The language we speak has to be different. We take language for granted. But I think language is an important tool to attract people to participate in something bigger. In the last few years NGOs have really spread here in Palestine and have brought their own language. Words like 'development' and 'strategic'. They're using language brought from the outside and the language is also occupying us and taking us away from our own language and vocabulary. Even people who don't speak English know what these NGO words mean.

Can you explain your critique of the word 'development'?

I don't like the word 'development' because it makes me feel that the third world countries are poor, ignorant, and backwards, that we need to work to catch up with the developed countries, 'the Western world'. These terms are forced upon us from the West and they were brought to us through international organisations who come with their agendas and opinions about us. They call us undeveloped countries. But we have a different way of living and culture. The way they talk about gender, violence, poverty, women. People coming with infrastructure projects and putting a sign up saying 'USAID': that's not developing. It's the opposite. But the funders won't fund a project if they can't put up their sign and their flag.

Can you talk more about the effect of Western NGOs on Palestinian society, and on farmers?

Working for an NGO is considered to be a good middle-class job. But if these NGOs are dependent on Western funds, they are normally funded by Western governments. Your project starts to depend on the agendas of these Western organisations, because most of it is conditional funding. Depending on international funds is first of all risky because it changes all the time depending on the priorities and crises that these international organisations are looking to support. If we accept funds even from governments that condemn us and our right to resist, and consider us terrorists, how can we change the reality and the power equation we are suffering from, so that the oppressed and the oppressor are equal?

USAID [the United States Agency for International Development] gave Palestinian farmers a new kind of cucumber. The small ones. They said, 'Here's the seeds, you don't have to pay anything.' The farmers tried it for the first season. The next year they said, 'You have to pay for the pesticide.' The following year they said that 'you have to pay for everything yourselves.' By this time the farmers were in so much debt, and the soil was not productive anymore. When everyone plants the same crop, that means they won't be able to sell it. In some cases [these USAID projects] have been done in collaboration with the Palestinian Ministry of Agriculture.

A similar thing happened [when Israel started occupying the West Bank] in 1967. Israel announced that all the resources of this land belong to the [Israeli] state, and they went to the Palestinian farmers and gave them seeds and chemicals and told them how to plant things. That's a way to control food, and also to gain control of our knowledge. Back then Palestinians were producing 80 percent of our needs and we were exporting sesame. Now we're importing almost all grains and legumes. What the Palestinian Authority spends on agriculture is less than 3 percent of the Gross Domestic Product (GDP)—it's nothing.

What is your position on accepting funding at Om Sleiman?

The farm started with a 'no fund' policy for the first three years, following that we decided to accept funds from local organisations, without conditions, to fund projects and education programmes. I think that when it comes to funds it's not black or white. The owner of the land gave us the land for free, isn't that some sort of funding? When we had an accident at the farm and lost all of our seed stock, we were able to recover our costs in a week because the community helped us right away, isn't it a sort of community fund? We see the importance of having the production side of the farm as self-sufficient, meaning that the membership fees paid by our customers for the price of vegetables should cover the cost of producing these crops. But other projects that we do could have a great effect on our nature and society. Why say no to individuals who want to donate to a project they feel proud of?

There are now more small farms [like Om Sleiman] and we try to share our skills because the others aren't organic or natural. They come and ask questions and see the results of our work. Maybe they will consider it when they go back to their farms.

We don't accept any type of funds that are conditioning us from doing what we believe we should do, also we feel it's important to not depend in any way on these sources of funding.

What is your financial model at Om Sleiman?

We are a community-supported agriculture farm, meaning that people sign up for the whole season, usually three months. They pay in advance in exchange for a weekly basket of our fresh organic produce. There is a direct relationship between consumers and us. We don't have to worry about marketing our produce, or getting money before we start the season. What members pay for is how much it costs us to grow. It might not be affordable for some people but we offer discounts and you can come and volunteer in exchange for produce as well. Having said that, I must share that producing vegetables is never enough to cover the costs of the farm, but we are not raising the prices because we want to be inclusive. What we try to do instead is to have other ways to increase our income through workshops, courses, selling dry herbs, etc.

What do you think of the international Boycott Divestment and Sanctions (BDS) movement?

I support the boycott movement, especially to influence the people abroad. One of the reasons why Israel is able to continue its occupation and brutality is because it is never held accountable for all the crimes it commits against us, even by international organisations whose job is to hold these regimes accountable and protect the rights of humans. Israel is mostly treated as if it's a normal country. If Israel is held accountable, things will be different. I support BDS but it shouldn't be the only way to resist, we should be able to resist in all the ways we choose.

What do you think about the factory farming of animals in Palestine?
Traditionally, people in Palestinian villages kept animals. But I don't think people are aware [of the realities] of factory farms: they imagine chickens running around freely. It's not like people visit the farms and see the thousands of chickens on top of each other. I don't think people make a connection between what they eat and the creature. When they order chicken, it's just meat. They don't think about the living creature who had a life span. But recently some consumers have started to be aware about the reality of where their food comes from. There is more and more demand for 'Baladi Eggs'—heirloom chicken eggs—and for [local] dairy products. I don't think the supply is enough and I don't think people really know what the animals they eat have been injected with.

Do you think people in Palestine have a strong connection to the land?
Of course, you try to take land from any group of people and they will hold tight to it and defend it with everything. We have a strong connection with the land because our land is occupied, because our land supplies us with everything we need, because we are a peasant community. I think the older generation, who worked on the land every day, know how precious it is and might appreciate it more.

Some people are trying to preserve the Palestinian natural heritage, like Vivien Sansour, she has a seed library and is very active in saving seeds and giving them to farmers.[1]

Later generations never worked on the land in the same way. I don't think you can love your land if you're neglecting it or using chemicals on it. The younger generation has other interests, especially those who grew up in the city with no chances to harvest or plant, and those growing up in villages are sent to universities to get a certificate and have a career. [There is a culture here that] even if you have no

---

1 Vivien Sansour is the founder of the Palestine Heirloom Seed Library. Her website states:

> The Palestine Heirloom Seed Library (PHSL) is an attempt to recover these ancient seeds and their stories and put them back into people's hands. The PHSL is an interactive art and agriculture project that aims to provide a conversation for people to exchange seeds and knowledge, and to tell the stories of food and agriculture that may have been buried away and waiting to sprout like a seed. It is also a place where visitors may feel inspired by the seed as a subversive rebel, of and for the people, travelling across borders and checkpoints to defy the violence of the landscape while reclaiming life and presence.

idea about what you want to learn, you go to university, graduate, get a master's, get married, have children. Most of the time you're told what to do by your parents, teachers, bosses. It's really hard to get out of this prison. I think it's applicable all over the world. It's really hard to get out of traditions, and you have to please everyone all the time. I know many people who are living a life that they have never chosen because they want to please people, or because they were too scared to try anything different.

Can you tell us about feminism in Palestine?
Here we have feminist women who don't even know they're feminist. Northwest of Ramallah there is a village called Deir Ballut. It has nine hundred dunams of land, managed by the women of the village.[2] It's all run by women. They plant, they weed, they seed, they harvest. For me this is feminist. Most of the men of the village go to work in the settlements and the women have to be responsible for covering the needs of their families.

The most vulnerable in society are those most affected by the different forms of restrictions and violence. Women, for example, face multilayered oppression starting from the patriarchal family construct until the dominating Israeli occupation. Palestinian women have always played a leading role, from resisting oppression through armed struggle to tending fields abandoned by men who left to earn an income working for Israelis. There is a misrepresentation and misperception of Arab and Muslim women by the West—they are seen as stripped from political participation but in reality they are political subjects. I invite you to see feminism in a different lens—the lens of a revolutionary Arab feminist, because in reality it's more radical than most white feminism.

2 A dunam, also known as a donum or dunum, was the Ottoman unit of land equivalent to the English acre, representing the amount of land that could be ploughed by a team of oxen in a day.

Mona Al-Farra

Mona is from Khan Younis, Gaza. She is a doctor who has spent her life working in grass-roots health organisations in Gaza, and has been involved in promoting community empowerment. We interviewed Mona in March 2021 via video call. In this interview, Mona describes the founding of Al-Awda Hospital in the 1990s. In May 2025, the Israeli military ordered the closure of the hospital, which was the last operational hospital in the northern Gaza Strip.

Where were you born and where did your family come from?
I was born in Khan Younis, which is a small town in the southern part of the Gaza Strip, and I lived all my life there until the age of seventeen, when I went to Cairo to get my first degree in medicine.

Was your family political?
Yes they were. My father was an elected member of the first Palestinian Legislative Council, and he participated in the resistance against the Zionist gangs in Palestine in 1948. I was first politicised by my family background and also the Israeli occupation of Palestine in 1967.

When did you become politically active?
I was thirteen years old [in 1967] when Israel occupied Gaza [as well as the West Bank, East Jerusalem, the Syrian Golan, and the Sinai]. The first month after the occupation started, there was resistance. I was in school at the time. I was part of the different demonstrations that took place against the occupation, despite my limited capacity as a young student. With my peers we did little things like distributing leaflets. At that time there were no printers—they were not allowed by

the occupation—so we took on small missions like copying the leaflets and making sure they were distributed. So this is what we did, and this was going on throughout the Gaza Strip. Some of my colleagues who were a bit older—like seventeen or eighteen—took part in the resistance as well by helping the freedom fighters in Gaza. Some of them were arrested. But we continued.

After that I went to Cairo to continue my studies, and I returned back after finishing my primary and secondary degrees. When I returned to Gaza, I joined the Union of Health Work Committees (UHWC), [now known as Al Awda Health and Community Association (AWDA)]. Since that time I'm very proud to say that I have always tried to be active within the community and within the UHWC.

How would you describe your politics now?

I vote left. I am a community activist addressing women and children's rights, via different grass-roots works. Empowering the community and supporting my people's steadfastness on the ground is my main goal. This is because I realise that the occupation's long-term strategy is to bring about another ethnic cleansing, by making life unbearable for Palestinian people in our land.

Can you tell us about the political significance of your medical work?

UHWC is a grass-roots health organisation based in Gaza. It was founded by a group of activists who are doctors, nurses, pharmacists, etc. When we began, we worked in the refugee camps and in the different parts of the Gaza Strip. At that time there was continuous confrontation between the people in Gaza and the Israeli occupation army. Part of our role as UHWC was to serve those who were injured and their families. Besides that, we aimed to serve the whole community, and our vision was to create medical infrastructure for a future Palestine, because we always thought that we were on the path toward freedom, self-determination, and getting our rights. Health must be considered among all this, and of course most of us are 'left' people, so our main vision is to fight privatisation of medicine and to make health services available for the people who need it, especially those who cannot afford even very small fees.

Through working with UHWC I had the privilege and honour to be part of a very radical group of men and women, and with them

I co-founded a hospital in Jabalia, called Al-Awda Hospital in 1993. 'Al-Awda' in English means 'return', because we as Palestinian people believe that the cornerstone of the Palestinian issue is of course the refugees.

What happened in Palestine in 1948, uprooting our people and destroying our villages, was a major ethnic cleansing process that made [hundreds of thousands of] Palestinian people homeless. They were replaced by Israeli Zionists and that's why we strongly believe that the right of return for Palestinian refugees is the main issue for us—as part of the process of self-determination and achieving our rights.

So our mission as doctors and health workers was not just about providing resources. We also had the vision that we were against privatisation and we were part of the political process in the region. We were part of this, within our vision, which is mainly a socialist vision.

After we founded Al-Awda Hospital, I had the idea of setting up health centres and centres for children. The aim of that was to promote health education—in the health centres—and to encourage children to read and do different activities like dancing, to keep the Palestinian culture and identity alive. We now have five centres, but in the beginning I founded only two. One such centre was in Jabalia refugee camp. Shahd [Abusalama, also interviewed for this book], her cousins, her brothers, and sisters were part of it. The centres were about more than healing; [they were also] about a message of solidarity with the people, with the refugees, with the political prisoners' families, and the families of people who lost their lives while fighting the occupation.

Later we set up another centre in Rafah, named after Rachel Corrie.[1] One of the purposes of the centre is to be a platform to connect people internationally who want to be in solidarity with Palestine, with our children.

I also played an important part in health education for women. I started a programme called Women Empowerment Through Health Education.

All of these projects I've mentioned are about community empowerment. My goal is still the same, supporting people's steadfastness on

1 Rachel Corrie was an American volunteer with the International Solidarity Movement (ISM). Rachel was crushed to death by an Israeli bulldozer while attempting to stop the demolition of a Palestinian home in Rafah, in 2003. She has become an icon of international solidarity among Palestinians.

the ground. I feel that this is part of my resistance against the occupation, because the occupation tries—by its different practices—to dehumanise us. It tries to make the environment very bad for our people, to encourage them to leave the country. I have always believed, and still believe, that our existence is resistance. That's why our people are entitled to have somebody, some organisations, to help them stay on the ground and to see to their needs: health, cultural, social, education, etc.

This is my means of resistance, this is how I resist the occupation. I cannot carry a weapon—not because I am weak or a coward—no, because I am older and I am a grandmother now and this is not for me. I believe that resistance is one of our rights according to international law, because we are occupied. Wherever you are occupied, you have the right to resist. When, where, and how is up to the Palestinian people to decide.

During the Second Intifada, the house where you grew up was destroyed by Israeli forces. What was the effect on you?

It had a big impact on me, and inspired me to continue my role as a health activist exposing the Israeli occupation's brutal acts against the people, like home demolitions, destruction of land, the uprooting of trees, and the killing of civilians during [four] major military attacks and many, many air raids. These amount to the continuous violation of human rights, including health. It goes beyond human rights violations. I consider them war crimes.

Do you relate to the word 'feminist'?

In the Palestinian case, we all suffer from the occupation, males and females. But the female suffering is doubled due to social and traditional constraints. In that sense I relate to feminism and support its movement.

What did your family do after their home was destroyed, where did they go?

My mother was living there [in the house which was demolished], she moved to live with me initially until she sorted out another place. I continued my life in Gaza and I'm still living in Gaza. I visit the UK to see my children who are living in Manchester, and I'm often invited to address communities in Scotland, England, and Ireland. I also receive many invitations to speak about my people in Australia, the US, and different countries. I carry a message from thousands of Palestinians who are living under the occupation, and educate people about us. Again, this is part of my activism and I believe it is very important because I manage to do a lot of networking with people in solidarity with Palestinian people.

This solidarity is a very important way of resisting the occupation. It helps our people because when I come back from my trips outside Gaza, I do another chain of visits telling the people on the ground that they are not alone and they are not forgotten. I tell them about the activities of groups in solidarity with the Palestinian people. I'm someone who is able to keep on moving from Gaza to the outside world, despite the difficulties of the siege, I manage in the end. I believe that through the years, the power of the solidarity movement has increased in the UK. It is not the same as ten or twenty years ago.

I think this is an important success for all of you who are in solidarity with Palestinian people. I believe the work is continuous because the struggle will continue even after we have got our rights. It is a long way off, but even after the end of the occupation, we have another battle, which is the struggle of working for social justice in Palestine, and globally as well. So we will continue working. Our activists here in Gaza or outside should not stop until justice prevails.

During the Israeli bombardments on Gaza in 2006, 2009, and 2014, you wrote a blog—*From Gaza with Love*—about the Israeli attacks. What made you begin to document the constant attacks on the Palestinians, and did you feel the world was listening?

I started my blog in 2006, but during the Second Intifada, which started in September 2000, I was continuously writing press releases, exposing the Israeli atrocities against the people. I especially wrote about the abuse of health rights from my position as a physician. So I started writing, writing, writing, sending press releases by email: stories about the children who came to the hospital who were attacked with flechettes [a type of ammunition fired from Israeli aircraft which release thousands of deadly darts], about the houses that were evacuated in the middle of the night, and about the continuous military incursions into Gaza. Before 2006, there was not a big assault but there were still daily atrocities against us.

I always felt that it was my duty to do this, to approach the Western, English-speaking world. And for me it was a way to express myself too. I felt good, rather than being worried all the time. Writing gave me the chance to feel that I was putting things on paper with a purpose. It was not just for fun, or a luxury.

After I started my blog I wrote more and more and, as I wrote, the atrocities increased as well. Then in 2009, there was a big attack against Gaza. I was in the UK at that moment, but I travelled home quickly to coordinate the medical relief for hospitals in Gaza, including at Al-Awda Hospital. The attack went on for twenty-three days. The attack in 2012 was shorter—like ten days—but it was very intense, hitting homes and terrorising innocent people. When Israeli forces want to target any part of the resistance, they don't care who is in the way. Human rights violations—war crimes—were so obvious. What is happening in the Occupied Territories, I call it war crimes with confidence. Those people who are responsible should be punished for what happened to my people over the years.

After that we had the 2014 attack. I was the deputy chair of the Red Crescent Society for the Gaza Strip, and I was also the head of a health committee. I stayed in the health centre for fifty-one continuous days, working until 7.00pm, interrupted by some ceasefire periods. I coordinated and organised all the health work at that centre. I can say a lot about it but I don't want to put in the details. It was a horror, it was a nightmare, and I myself was caught in the fire twice but I escaped being killed. Israeli forces targeted hospitals, they targeted schools.

After that I received many, many calls asking me to tell the world about what's happening in Gaza. This is very important because I am not a journalist, but I am a human being talking from my firsthand experience, so my message was from the heart and from experience. The attack was very underreported. I feel sometimes that what we have experienced is not covered well. Right up to this minute we are under daily attack—small attacks. But for the world to notice—to talk about us—they need to see a lot of bloodshed.

Here in Gaza 2.2 million of us are attacked nearly daily, and daily there are attacks on farmers who are just trying to go to their land, or on the fisherman who are trying to fish. At the moment most of the people in Gaza are in a dire situation.

I'd like to mention something before I forget. And that is that the BDS movement has done very well. I work within the Palestinian NGO Network (PNGO) to encourage people here in Gaza, in hospitals and in medical facilities to boycott Israeli companies and we have succeeded a great deal. But sometimes we use Israeli products when there is no local alternative, because we are under occupation.

You have been involved in several movements to break the Israeli blockade from within and externally, with international support. How successful do you think these movements have been?
I believe they were very successful. They contributed to more awareness among Western people about our cause, about the occupation, and Gaza siege. They were a big act of solidarity, and a chance to expand the solidarity movement. The most important and unique one was the boats to Gaza.

What was your experience during the 2018–19 Great March of Return protests? And how was the international response to the movement?
I was on my way back to Gaza when the marches began. I met the Great March of Return members who were trying to enter from outside in Cairo, and I helped with the Palestinian NGOs network statement. But in the end, the Egyptians did not allow the majority of activists to enter Gaza. I met marvellous comrades in Cairo. We tried to travel via Rafah, but we were not allowed through by the Egyptian authorities. In the end these people couldn't enter. I carried eight bags of aid with me to Gaza—medicine mainly—and entered alone after a few tries.

During the Great March of Return, Ahmed Abu Artema—one of the prominent organisers of the March—made public calls for One Democratic State in all of historic Palestine [Gaza, the West Bank, and Israel—Palestine before the creation of Israel], with equality for Palestinians and Israelis. What do you think of these calls for One Democratic State?
This is the future inevitable solution, that will be based on justice and return, as well as long-term prosperity, stability, justice, and peace. It will take time, a very long time, but it will happen as long as there is international will to address peace and justice in Palestine.

What has been your experience during the COVID-19 pandemic?
Our life under occupation has never been, and is still not, easy. It is a daily struggle even for the basic things. Now we are living through the COVID-19 [pandemic]. Civil society organisations have sent many letters explaining how at the moment—and through this pandemic—we are experiencing a new type of apartheid. I call it health apartheid. In the beginning of the pandemic, no medicine could enter Gaza. Then there was some negotiation and compromise to allow medicine to enter Gaza, but only if the resistance here accepted the constraints put on them by the Israeli military.

It shouldn't be like that, because having accessibility to health and medicine is a basic human right for people according to the Geneva Convention—this is number one. Number two, just a couple of days ago, after big negotiations, they did not allow the first two thousand shots of the Coronavirus vaccine to enter Gaza. Now they have allowed the vaccines to enter Gaza, and in another two weeks we will have another ten thousand shots. But compared to the needs of the population, this is a very small amount, and there are always obstacles.

When you look at the other side, Israel has managed to give the vaccine to at least four million of its [eight million] population. This is a very high number compared to other Western countries like Britain and the US. But still they are bargaining with us about letting in a few thousand vaccines for our population. This is discrimination, a war crime—when you use health for political reasons.

Me, myself, I'm not surprised because we are dealing with an occupying, colonial, racist, and apartheid regime. It's a big shame for the world that this so-called democracy is existing in the ruins of other people, who are the original people of the land.

Can you tell us about the work you do now, and its political significance?
I am now the MECA [Middle East Children's Alliance] Projects Director in Gaza. I design different projects with my team and community-based organisations. These include projects on health, water, and culture to help keep Palestinian heritage and identity alive. Educational, aid, and psychological support via different creative activities. Our work also includes creating playing fields for young women and the community and encouraging cycling and other sports.

These activities are politically supporting people's existence on the land, and I also make many links with international political solidarity groups. I update them on the current situation, and convey their message of solidarity from the outside world to Palestine. This message helps my people's psychological well-being, to know that we are not alone and never forgotten. I am convinced that this work is politics, and resistance too.

Are you hopeful about the global political situation and its impact on Gaza?
At the moment, no. But I strongly believe in inevitable world political changes. The Berlin Wall collapsed in a day, the Soviet Union too. Apartheid in South Africa is now part of history. The future will bring up many world changes and we will never give up our activism and political work toward our different causes, including Palestine.

How hopeful are you about the political situation within Gaza?
I am not hopeful now.

What is your biggest hope when it comes to Palestinian freedom?
For the return of the refugees and One Democratic State.

What do you think the world that you are struggling for looks like?
Socialism and social justice.

What keeps you going when you feel at your lowest?
Ordinary people in Palestine. Those women, men, and children who are struggling daily and never give up under all the difficult circumstances, and endure a great deal of deprivation and injustice.

What would be your advice to younger Palestinian women who want to make change in Gaza?
Firstly, to believe in themselves as women living under occupation, to believe that they are strong enough to make real change in shaping our future. Secondly, to have clear and focused goals. Thirdly, to work on long-term goals too. Fourthly, to give time to politics and community voluntary work; it has great value in their empowerment, they will realise that later on. And also to learn how it is important to work

within a team and to accept differences. To be confident in themselves, to learn more about global struggles. And lastly reading, reading, and more reading.

What is very important to me as a woman who has spent all my life in this struggle is to pass on the message to younger generations. This is what I am doing now, trying to inspire other people. Because the youth are the future and the work is continuous. This is part of our strength as Palestinians, because we are still on the land. In Gaza we are 2.2 million, in the West Bank, 3 million, and we are keeping the culture and habits.

What they are trying to do in Gaza is a new kind of genocide. Part of that genocide is that they want to destroy our culture, our heritage. Me and my comrades, we want to keep the Palestinian identity alive, and not to allow them to crush us with their boots.

Mona Al-Farra (2025 Update)

Mona is from Khan Younis, Gaza. She is currently living in Manchester, UK. Mona arrived in the UK to be near her children one month after Israel's latest assault on Gaza began in October 2023. She told us that she sometimes feels 'survivor's guilt' when she thinks about what's happening back home. We interviewed Mona a second time in August 2024, over the phone, and she sent us further comments in January 2025, days before the announcement of a temporary ceasefire in Gaza.

How is your family in Gaza?

I have family in Khan Younis, but everyone in Gaza is my family. It is difficult when things are personal—I've lost many second, third cousins, maybe up to 255 now, and every day I hear sad news about losses. Facebook has changed to a page of condolences about the lost people that I love, worked with, who were part of my community. A couple of days ago, the son of my colleague, who is a dentist, was killed. He was only twenty-eight, and he was delivering basic food in northern Gaza to the displaced people at one of the schools. He was killed with his friend. This is just one example. In the meantime I don't give up on what I'm doing. It's not only about family, but about everyone in Gaza.

On a daily basis I am in touch with comrades in Gaza—this is very draining but I cannot help but do it because I know that when we talk together they have some relief hearing my voice. I feel the same too. It's nothing compared to what they are facing. Despite that, I try to work while I am in the UK, and I join protests. Last week I went to a demonstration at an arms factory in Blackburn [BAE Systems], where

F-35 jets are manufactured and sent to the Israeli military. When I saw the F-35s for the first time so close, I felt rage and had flashbacks to all the times I've heard the horrible sounds of these planes, and how many bombs they have dropped on Gaza.

The protesting crowd was there. It was uplifting to see the solidarity with Palestinian people, but still it was not a good experience for me, to be in touch with this monster—to see it for the first time in my life so close-up. If I was young, like sixteen or seventeen, I wouldn't be able to help but climb the wire fence around the weapons factory. As you get older though, health does not help, as well as wisdom with what's happening here in the UK too—people who are in the demonstrations are under severe surveillance all the time.

How easy has it been to communicate with people back home?
Communication is not easy, it is rare. It is there, but it's not on a regular basis because the internet either gets cut off or interrupted. When people do have internet, it's dangerous for them to go to where there is a signal. Snipers are on the roofs in Gaza City, for example. Sometimes friends will walk two kilometres, in a very dangerous situation just to get in touch and say, 'We are alive and please continue what you are all doing in Britain.' They want to follow the solidarity movement in Britain and elsewhere, via people like me and others too. I think this is very important for many reasons. First to support the people that I know in Gaza—they are all activists and people who are volunteering now. There is a network delivering food, medicine, and assistance for the people. I convey the message, making the link between them and what's going on in the UK. It's crucial that the non-stop demonstrations and protests are heard in Gaza, it helps people to know they are not alone; they are not forgotten, despite all that is happening regarding the complicity of some Arab countries with the US and the UK, against our own country.

Life is so cruel at the moment, it's unbelievable what is happening. I try not to lose our compass when saying that it's not about October 7, it's about the history of Zionism and the way Israel was founded. It's not isolated from the capitalist and colonial systems. This is not just about Palestine—what's happening in Palestine intensifies the injustice that is happening all over the world.

The UK is so connected to what is happening in Palestine, and elsewhere, because of its connection to these wider colonial systems. How do you feel about being in the belly of the beast during this time?
It's not easy and it is stressful too. I don't feel absolutely satisfied or at peace because there are many who either don't want to know, or they know and they are not on the right side of life. There are also others who believe in the system here and the government. The UK government is failing its own people by continuing these arms deals with Israel, but some people don't want to listen because of the media here, especially the mainstream media. People don't have time to listen or to try to understand, and that's why I try to tell our story in a clear way, because the media is very much against us.

What brings me peace is that I'm surrounded by people in solidarity. In Manchester there are vigils at every small street corner. I feel uplifted to see Palestinian flags. That means a lot for me and I hope that one day these voices for peace and justice in Palestine will be heard. I'm not naive—I don't think it's going to be very soon, it will take time, but people change, and people will change the governments. It takes a lot of solidarity and effort, but I don't lose this hope for the future. I'm not being romantic or unrealistic; I know it will take time and being together to be united for one goal.

I'm inspired by apartheid falling in South Africa, I'm inspired by other people's struggles against imperialism. But after what's happened in Gaza, I'm not the same person, because I feel rage and anger, like all of you. What's happening is genocide, it is beyond the imagination.

What was it like in Gaza before October 7?
I was not surprised by October 7 because it was boiling under the surface. It is about the occupation, siege, and injustice.

It is not about October 7, it is the ongoing injustice that has been imposed on my people since the ethnic cleansing of Palestine [in 1948], and the replacement of Palestine by Israel.

In Gaza just before October 7, unemployment was very high, poverty, poor nutrition, and health problems—nothing was in a good shape. The situation was really deteriorating. The siege was continuing, hundreds of thousands of youths left for a new life outside Gaza, and we expected it would explode at some point. We didn't expect it would happen this way though, and nobody expected this size of reaction from the Israeli army, or for the Israeli government to reach the level of genocide. There is also famine in a lot of the Gaza Strip, people can't find food to eat.

What's been happening to healthcare in Gaza since the start of the genocide?

My ex-husband is a doctor, he runs an IVF centre in Gaza. He lost everything. In the centre there were frozen embryos that were killed as well. They were for parents who cannot conceive.

They are destroying healthcare in Gaza in a systematic way. At least one thousand health workers, including doctors and other health professionals, have been killed, thousands have been injured, have become disabled, and many are imprisoned. Some have been killed during torture. Every day I think of my colleagues who are imprisoned. A big issue is that they are treated cruelly inside the jails with a lack of food, lack of medical care, they are not allowed visits, and they cannot see their relatives. Also, the doctors that have died under torture—two cases have been reported—one is doctor Dr Adnan al-Bursh and the other is Dr Iyad al-Rantisi.

The hospital that I co-founded in Jabalia refugee camp with my colleagues a long time ago is called Al-Awda Hospital. The director of the hospital is one of six health professionals [from Al-Awda] who are in jail. We haven't had any information about where they are since the end of December 2023, up until today. This is a small example. The same has happened to other hospitals inside the same camp, like Kamal Adwan Hospital and the Indonesian Hospital.

All what is happening to people's health makes me very angry and sad: the destruction of frozen embryos, the outbreak of poliomyelitis, the famine and severe shortage of medications, either on a primary health or secondary health level. It means more people die every day as an outcome of the continuing genocide. These include eight newborn babies that died inside the displaced people's tents due to the severely cold weather, not to forget the premature babies who died in the beginning of the genocide and more recently, after Kamal Adwan Hospital was completely destroyed.

It took such a long time until this first case of poliomyelitis was recorded and there's been no vaccinations to date. The electricity situation is bad, so I'm not sure if the vaccine will be able to prevent the spread of the disease completely, because the vaccine needs to be kept at a specific temperature. Of course it's not only poliomyelitis, but the spread of hepatitis C, and the lack of water. All health has been affected a great deal. Health means life, and destruction of the healthcare of any nation is a war crime.

What do your colleagues in Gaza—healthcare workers—need the most right now?

First they need protection while working, either inside the hospitals or while evacuating the dead. They also need medicine, as the most basic medicine in Gaza, like painkillers, is lacking. They need reliable oxygen supplies, medical supplies, and equipment. Everything has been destroyed so the hospitals are working at very low capacity. We also need to support the workers who are working around the clock, who have lost everything, who have lost their people like everyone else. Financially they will be suffering—they are working voluntarily. We need to tell the world their stories and to support them as people as well. The hospitals also need fuel and food, everything is needed.

Doctors have lost their lives. Many of them are highly skilled, specialised consultants. This has all disappeared now. If there is a ceasefire there would need to be other stages—the first stage we are doing now is providing aid for people and saving lives, the second stage will be the rehabilitation of the health system, slowly, and the third stage has to be to deliver all the services that were already lacking in Gaza [before the start of Israel's genocide].

Another thing I would like to mention is that cancer patients are dying every day, as well as the renal dialysis patients. People are dying. Everything is lacking. I don't like to keep mentioning the lists.

In spite of all that there are still flashes of light. In the displaced schools, for example, you will find volunteers—youth—running activities for young children: singing, dancing, educating, and telling stories while under attack.

Those volunteers are the outcome of many years of work by my organisation and others. We implement projects and train youth how to deal with traumatised children, so this is something to thank all the relevant organisations and non-governmental organisations for. It shows the steadfastness of the Palestinian people and the feeling that we are not victims, we are freedom fighters.

Do you think Israel has been deliberately targeting surgeons and other health workers?

Yes, they are destroying every single detail of Palestinian people's lives in Gaza, and by destroying the health system people will start dying slowly because of a lack of services, so it is part of the genocide. Killing the health workers, it's a big crime. They kill them so that people die from disease or their injuries. They destroy the hospitals and, again, the consequence of that is a lack of services.

They destroy the water wells so there will not be enough clean water, and of course this will have an effect on health and well-being. This is the killing of people indirectly—this is genocide. There is not enough aid entering Gaza. Every single person has lost at least ten to fifteen kilograms in weight. It's not only genocide, it's a new concentration camp, a new version of the concentration camps.

All the people of the world say that what Nazis did should never happen again, and it's happening now, committed by the grandchildren of the Holocaust victims. They try all the time to say, 'It's for security and Israel has the right to defend itself', but this is not Israel defending itself, it's destruction and racism and I can see the link between this and the concentration camps. It's a sensitive issue but I'm not afraid of saying it, and it's time they stopped intimidating people by saying they're antisemitic. It's not about antisemitism, it's about war crimes, whoever it is doing it.

What are your thoughts on how the international community has been responding to this genocide?

The international community is great—the people, that is—non-stop demonstrations in every part of the world. And the students' encampments, despite the fact that the police managed to stop them. This is the normal reaction of humans, whether they are political or non-political, to be against the killing. So I think it has been great, but I also see that it is not enough, because there are still people who don't want to know anything about us, or they just close their eyes. These are individualistic people, who just want to carry on with their lives. You find them everywhere in the world, but I'm proud of what's happening in solidarity, and against what's happening in Gaza.

I feel shame about the Arab and Islamic governments. They did not allow their people to express their feelings about Gaza, to the extent that people were put in jail if they wanted to have a demonstration. I'm very ashamed of this situation. These governments are accomplices with Israel and America. Because they are puppets, they are capitalists, and they don't care about their people. They care about their thrones—their kingdoms or republics—and they are puppets of America because they are capitalists themselves.

When we spoke before, you mentioned supporting the campaign for One Democratic State in all historic Palestine. How do you feel about the prospects for One Democratic State now, after everything that's happened over the past year?

While the Americans and British and everybody are talking about a two-state solution, this is really nonsense. There's been no place for a two-state solution for a long time. But now, with the current situation, there is no place at all. The answer was, and still is—in my opinion—that Palestine should be free from the river to the sea. And this means the whole land and the whole people, including the Israeli people, should share this land, based on one democratic state for all. And when we say that Palestine will be free from the river to the sea, that means there's another battle—the liberation of the Israeli people from the racist and colonial Zionist ideology. The Palestinian people will never ever give up their right of return and their independence.

The circumstances have proved that the existence of even a small piece of land is resistance, and the Palestinians will never be defeated or taken for granted. Since October 7, the Israelis have created a more radical generation. Those who have witnessed what has happened since October 7 in Gaza will be more radical than the previous generations. The answer is—more than at any time—that the solution should be one state for all.

What strategies do you think we can use to end the genocide?

The strategy should be to continue what we are doing, and not give up because our voices will be heard regarding the rights of Palestinian people. One day the governments will have the time to listen to the people, because we are together on the right path of life and things change. This is history—nothing stays the same. As long as we do not vanish as Palestinian people, and we will not vanish because we have great support from people all over the world—people who believe in rights, freedom, liberty, equality. This is the strategy, to continue and always find new ways of struggling so people don't feel burnt out— by that I mean the people outside of Palestine.

I am very impressed in Britain to see many younger people supporting this movement. This gives me hope as well. But politically, things like talks or negotiations [sighs], I don't know what to say. It's important that people are there and the movement is getting bigger, and all the time finding ways of telling the story in a less complicated way. Keep the flame. Like what you are doing now—by compiling this book—what you are doing is extremely important.

There are many cultural activities here in Manchester—poems, singing, plays—all informing people about Palestinian heritage. Writing is also a very important tool. Also sports—for example, in Manchester there's a Big Ride for Palestine, that has also been happening all over Britain, I am one of the founders. I did part of the ride myself, but I had to stop after I had an accident. This year it was a great success and all the proceeds will go to our projects in Gaza. There is another organisation called Gaza Sunbirds—they deal with amputees, sports for amputees. I'm very proud of it.

There is another group now in Manchester that my son founded with his friend, it's called Amplify Gaza Stories. My son stayed in Gaza for two months after October 7, so he has connections there. They have stories from Gaza and they amplify the stories and make cartoons as well sometimes, animations too. They raise money and they send it to the people for co-operative kitchens—a way of empowerment for the families, for the community, with the support of Amplify Gaza Stories. They call it a co-operative, because it's not the way of charity, [not a charity model]. They try to develop people and help people.

Is there anything else you would like to add?

Every single person in Gaza has lost something. The majority have lost homes, including myself and my family—my house, my sister's, my brother's, my parents' family house. And there's the number who have been killed, a huge number including women and children. Agricultural land has been destroyed. Every single human being has been affected by this genocide in one way or another.

The effects of this will continue for many years, and we still don't know what the real goal for the Israelis is. But the most heartbreaking thing is the displacement. Those people who are displaced and have been squeezed into just 11 percent of Gaza's land. There are 1.8 million people squeezed into 11 percent of the land. I say concentration camp because it is one tent next to the other, and every day they [the Israeli military] give them new instructions to leave for another place—squeeze, squeeze—and they are not safe in these displaced places; they keep hitting them with air strikes.

It's very ugly, very cruel, very inhuman. Israel, the so-called only democracy in the Middle East, this is what they are doing. And the effect on the children will live with them for many years to come, the trauma, the effects on people's health, their education, the social fabric of the community. Despite the solidarity and the steadfastness, such situations will make people impatient, will make people angry and quarrelsome. This is normal, we are human beings. Of course I say that we are steadfast, and that is the case, but in the end it is people, ordinary people just bumping into each other in crowded, small places.

One day when this is mentioned in history people shouldn't say 'we never knew'—because the media was there. It's not like the previous century. People should not say 'we did not know that this was happening'—they knew, but they did not want to intervene. Or some of them did not want to know, and this is a shame for the whole of humanity. Humanity has been failed and Gaza has been failed by the people who are not active in their solidarity with the Palestinian people.

Faiza Abu Shamsiyah

Faiza is from Al-Khalil/Hebron in the West Bank, where she is an activist and video journalist. She lives in Tel Rumeida, a neighbourhood very close to several Israeli colonies inhabited by extremely violent settlers. Approximately two thousand Israeli soldiers are stationed close by, ostensibly to protect the roughly seven hundred settlers. Like every Palestinian family in Tel Rumeida, Faiza's family encounters daily acts of harassment and violence from the Israeli military. We interviewed Faiza in August 2018, in a municipality building in Al-Khalil.

Can you tell us about yourself?

I'm a resident of Tel Rumeida in Hebron, and I'm a mother of five children as well as an employee of the Hebron governorate office. I'm also a woman activist, and a video journalist with Human Rights Defenders. I document the killing of women at the Women's Centre for Legal Aid and Counselling, a Palestinian NGO which works all over the West Bank.

I have been a video journalist since 2010. My first experience of filming was with B'Tselem [an Israeli human rights organisation]. After settlers attacked my daughter, B'Tselem supplied the family with cameras and I began to volunteer with them. My daughter was going to school earlier than normal because she had an additional class, so she left the house at 6.00am. There were three or four settlers passing by at the same time and they set their dog on her to attack her. She ran away. While my daughter was running, she fell and broke her jaw. She was taken to hospital and she was unconscious for two days.

I met B'Tselem volunteers and they collected statements. They suggested that I take a camera. In the beginning I refused. I said, 'I cannot film.' But my husband said, 'Take the camera and I'll train you how to use it'. When I first started, sometimes my pictures weren't level and sometimes I forgot to open the lens! My husband also encouraged me not to be afraid of being attacked by the settlers.

Another trainer from B'Tselem gave us a workshop about safety while filming. Then I became more used to it. The camera was important because it reduced the number of settler attacks on my family. The settlers knew we had cameras. They used to attack me and try to break my camera, try to take the memory card, and sometimes soldiers came up to me to prevent me from filming. Every time I filmed I was restricted, but this made me stronger. Then I started going out and filming if my neighbours were attacked. Sometimes I would document the clashes [between stone-throwing Palestinians and the army] on the streets. I like using the camera to reveal the crimes of the occupation.

Can you tell us about Human Rights Defenders?

Tel Rumeida was closed [by the Israeli military] in 2000, after the Second Intifada began. On November 1, 2015, after the assassination of Hadeel [al-Hashlamon, an eighteen-year-old woman who was killed by an Israeli soldier on September 22, 2015], the closure was further emphasised and became a lot harder, with specific IDs given to the people of the neighbourhood. Everyone else was banned from entering.[1]

The Israeli military prevented the media from coming into the neighbourhood. So we started filming things by ourselves and we formed the National Association of Human Rights Defenders in 2017. We have around twenty-three Palestinians volunteering with cameras and lots of international activists. Human Rights Defenders (HRD) has also trained children to film in schools which are close to settlers and the army. The group doesn't just film in Tel Rumeida, but close to the settler enclaves around Kiryat Arba.

Now people who film footage with their phones also give us their videos. And we have a group of women in Gaza who are cooperating

1 In 2015, Hebron's Palestinians came under very heavy violence from Israeli forces after the outbreak of a new Palestinian uprising against the occupation.

with us too. We exchange footage and we talk about our suffering. We have good relations with B'Tselem and sometimes we give them footage. But we felt that B'Tselem's attention on the area had decreased, and sometimes they didn't take our videos and publish them. Despite this the coordinator of B'Tselem is still my hero and I still follow what she does.

Our main goal is to expose the crimes of the occupation and we're open to cooperating with everyone. It's become a phenomenon now—everyone holds their phone and starts filming. But with B'Tselem there we feel more protected because it's an Israeli NGO and has a big name. This gives us some protection because we work alongside them. If you don't praise the people who help you, you don't praise God! We appreciate B'Tselem's support but we feel that a Palestinian-led body is necessary and deserves support from others. There is a difference between those who live such reality and those who observe it. And what motivates our work is the spirit of belonging and survival.

We know that Israeli violations are not limited to 9.00am to 5.00pm on weekdays. Such assaults can happen at any time. If Israeli forces break into our house at 2.00am, who's going to defend us? Therefore, through Human Rights Defenders, we feel more empowered, we have control on our narrative and we expose our lived reality as it is, with no filters. Currently, due to the pandemic and Israeli military restrictions on who enters the military zone, our relations with B'Tselem are not as strong as before. But we keep on going. We called our first filming project in 2017, the Capturing the Occupation Camera Project.

A renowned Palestinian activist, Badee Dweik, is involved with Human Rights Defenders. We started with very humble means, but we were determined to do this as it was about life and death. We also did it for the sake of history, to keep things on record. The International Solidarity Movement branch in northern California was monumental in helping us, providing cameras and laptops to help us found HRD.[2]

Ever since, we have been distributing those cameras to the families of Tel Rumeida and training children and their parents on how to

2 The International Solidarity Movement (https://palsolidarity.org) was founded during the Second Palestinian Intifada. It aims to support Palestinian grass-roots resistance to the Israeli occupation.

use them in a safe and effective way. For example, we advise them to remain twenty-five metres away from the violent events they witness, a distance that is sometimes hard to achieve when people themselves are at the centre of the violence, but we do our best.

How is it as a woman, doing your job?

In the beginning I was worried about what people would say about me in Palestinian society. But I'm a strong woman and I have learnt to challenge everything. My neighbours started calling me if they were being attacked by settlers. Many of the women want to join us and film, but they're worried about whether the settlers will attack them. I've started encouraging them and raising their spirits.

As a Palestinian woman I try to focus more on how the children and women suffer. I also try to encourage women to go and visit the Ibrahimi Mosque: they don't want to go because of the checkpoints [which surround the mosque]. I take them to eat breakfast in the old city or pray in the mosque.

Can you talk more about the hassle your family gets from the settlers and soldiers in Tel Rumeida?

Sometimes I will go and film settlers and they run away. But sometimes they try to beat up my children or throw trash onto my house [roof], or go onto my roof and pee down onto the house. They even burnt part of my house, and they poisoned the water tanks on my roof. One time we wanted to be sure that the water tanks were clean, and my daughter went up to check them. Five settlers came to the roof and chased her to the edge and then pushed her. On another occasion she was walking home from school and they burnt her hair. She was only seven years old at the time. She had psychological issues because of these experiences, and Médecins Sans Frontières treated her.

My youngest boy was stabbed once in his arm and this was documented on video. He was detained for four or five hours by the Israeli military when he was nine years old and put in complete isolation. My oldest son, Awni, has been the most harassed. In 2013, Awni was beaten. And on December 22, 2015, he was shot in both his legs on the hilltop in Tel Rumeida. The settlers used to target Awni as a way to get revenge on the whole family [for remaining in Tel Rumeida, and for their work with B'Tselem and Human Rights Defenders]. As of April

2021, Awni is currently banned from entering the closed military zone. In early 2021, the military court issued an order to prevent Awni from entering Tel Rumeida until 2023.

Madelin, my daughter, was once forced to stay indoors for fifteen days because she was directly threatened by a female settler. Another time, Madelin was detained for three hours with a couple of other girls and interrogated by the Israeli police. After that, two Israeli police officers came to our home and accused Madelin of throwing rocks at settlers. The police officers said that 'for her own safety' she should stay indoors for two weeks.

The same thing happened to me in 2019. I was put under house arrest for two weeks. The whole story behind it is ridiculous. On October 31, 2019, Awni and I had just returned from Jordan; Awni had three operations on his legs [in Jordan] after he was shot by the settlers. Some visitors came to check on us. Soon after, Israeli soldiers broke into the house. Their excuse was that they had got news that some Palestinians had been smuggled illegally into Tel Rumeida. I stood up to challenge them and protect my son and visitors, and they arrested me and interrogated me. Eventually they accused me of 'disrupting soldiers at work' and put me under home arrest. This is just some of [mine and] my children's suffering, but all of the families in my neighbourhood suffer, and every household has their own story.

Does having a camera with you reduce harassment from soldiers and settlers?

If soldiers behave in a rude way, having a camera there can reduce that. The soldiers now look around and check whether people are filming. In certain incidents, the footage has shown the truth and that has helped a lot of people. We send someone to film the action. But we also send someone to film the filming, taking different angles. I know of about ten cases where the Israelis were going to make a fraudulent claim [against Palestinians] or where Israeli forces had detained people. But these people were released before arrest because of the cameras filming. [In Hebron, and elsewhere in Palestine, it is common for Palestinians to be detained blindfolded on the street by Israeli soldiers, before either being arrested or released.]

All these documented events are published on Human Rights Defenders' Facebook page, and the YouTube channel of the Capturing the Occupation Camera Project. We currently have more than two thousand hours of film of real events that we encounter and we encourage filmmakers and international human rights defenders to get in touch in order to put these filmed events to effective public use.

In 2018, I was drying my laundry and one of the Israeli soldiers who were stationed on our home's rooftop started blowing me kisses. So I started filming. At the same time my son, Saleh, was coming home, and the soldier started bothering him. My son came into the house, but then the soldiers came round, saying that they wanted to take him. The same soldier who had been blowing me kisses had told his colleagues that Saleh had been throwing rocks at him. DCO officers then came, DCO stands for District Coordination Office, [which are] Israeli-Palestinian military coordination offices established as part of the 1994 Gaza-Jericho Agreement between Israel and the Palestinian Authority.

I told the officers that the soldiers were coming to arrest my son, but that he didn't throw rocks. I told them that the soldier was trying to flirt and that this was against our custom. The DCO saw my footage and Saleh wasn't arrested. The soldier was told to go to the military base, and later I saw him sweeping the street. He came and apologised to me, saying that he thought he had been greeting me, not flirting. The DCO said that I could complain to the police, although I haven't. This is life for Palestinian women under the occupation.

In March 2016, two young Palestinian men, Ramzi al-Qasrawi and Abdul Fattah al-Sharif, were murdered by Israeli soldier Elor Azaria. Your husband Imad filmed the moment when Azaria shot al-Sharif in the head. Can you tell us about that day?

That day, the children went to school and workers came to renovate the house. I made them coffee, but we couldn't drink it because we heard shooting. I went outside very quickly. There was a Palestinian worker on our roof and he said that the soldiers had shot somebody. Imad went out with bare feet. I carried the camera and went out after my husband. My husband shouted, 'They shot him!' I gave him the camera. The man was lying on the ground and moving a little bit. I was saying, 'He's alive.' A mother's feeling is very strong. I started shouting at the soldiers, 'He's my brother, he's my neighbour.' This attracted the attention of the soldiers, so I told Imad to go and film elsewhere. The soldiers pulled me out from behind the wall and two soldiers held onto each of my hands. I noticed that my husband was on our neighbour's roof, and he shook his head, indicating to me not to tell the soldiers where he was.

When Imad was on the neighbour's roof, one of the soldiers moved the man with his foot. I said, 'You should be merciful, he is still alive.' The soldiers said, 'He is a terrorist.' The soldier was saying that he had a suicide belt on and I said, 'No, let me approach him.' [The soldiers then shot him dead.] Imad filmed from the roof and revealed the crime. May God be merciful on the victim. It was a Jewish holiday—Purim—and the soldiers brought water tanks over and washed the blood from the street. Annette Cohen [a notoriously violent religious settler] was giving sweets to the soldiers to celebrate the killing.

There is footage of the murderer, Elor Azaria, shaking hands with Baruch Marzel and Ofer Ohana [the medic who moved a knife closer to the body].[3] Baruch leads a settler movement [and is a right-wing extremist politician], and was a close friend and colleague of Baruch Goldstein who committed the massacre in the Ibrahimi Mosque, killing fifteen Palestinians during Ramadan in 1994. Ofer is an infamous settler paramedic [whose violence has been exposed by Palestinians] and he has been banished from his work as a result.

After the shooting, Imad was shocked. It was hard for him to believe that he had filmed the death. We started having lots of phone calls. My phone was ringing constantly with people wanting to know about the incident. It spread very quickly. For a month I was afraid. I had seen them executing him. I was worried about my family, and told my husband that we should live somewhere else. My husband received death threats and we were threatened with being burnt.

---

3 In 2021, Ofer—the same Israeli colonist mentioned in this interview—shot a Palestinian woman dead in Hebron. Her name was Wafa' Abdul-Rahim Barade'ey. Independent Middle East Media Center wrote at the time:

> An Israeli military spokesperson tried to claim that the Palestinian woman was armed and had opened fire with an M-16 rifle, and some Israeli media outlets took the narrative for granted and even reported the incident was an attempted stabbing attack, pictures from the scene show the woman posed no threat to the soldiers, or anybody else. What they show is an armed paramilitary settler taking a knee to aim before killing her. The gun he used is then seen planted near her body, as if she had been the one holding it.

See https://imemc.org/article/israeli-colonist-kills-a-palestinian-woman-in-hebron.

After the murder, the Israeli soldiers closed the area more tightly. Until now we are denied visitors under military order. At the end of Ramadan, the family usually visits each other in our homes, but this year my family cannot visit anyone. For two years [following 2015], we were treated like numbers. Israeli soldiers issued special IDs with numbers allocated to each Palestinian who lives in the neighbourhood. We would be called by numbers, not names, as if we were not humans. At checkpoints, soldiers would say, for example, 'Number twenty is allowed, but number sixty-six (my number) is not allowed.' It was horrible, and every time they changed the Israeli forces operating in the area, they would change our numbers. If our numbers weren't detected at the checkpoint, because of a technical error they made, they would turn our lives into hell.

Can you talk more about the psychological impact of life under occupation, especially for women and children?

Our suffering is endless under the occupation. During a night raid, they confiscated my kitchen knives. Now I have to smuggle in small knives for peeling oranges. Our children become irritated. When will children have their freedom to play here? Our children play in the street and don't have a playground, and the soldiers grab their footballs and destroy them. Palestinian children all go and buy toy guns. It's forbidden by the occupation for our children to fly kites. The children have bikes and they want to take them out, but the soldiers won't open the side gate of the checkpoint to let them through. The army sometimes confiscates the kids' bikes. I once videoed soldiers taking the ball of a child and putting it inside their checkpoint.

Children can't carry compasses to school because they're banned by the Israelis. They have to keep them at school. I want to launch a campaign for the children, to talk about their rights and their suffering. I want to give them toys to play with in the streets. It's a basic right for children. Where should the children go to play here? There is a community centre in the south part of the city with a swimming pool, but we need to pass at least three checkpoints to go to that place.

I am worried all the time. Every time I pass these checkpoints I risk my life. But I don't want to restrict myself and I don't want my girls to be shy. I don't want them to be stuck in the house. I want them to have pride and the will for freedom. I want them to believe that we will achieve that. I want them to be brave. But I have less control over my boys. My son, Saleh, is fond of videoing. He's holding the camera all the time. And at least half of the soldiers know his name.

One high school girl was on her period and had sanitary pads in her bag. The soldiers wanted to force her to put everything on the table [at a checkpoint]. This is very sensitive in our culture. Now, every time she is on her period she won't go to school. Her mother explained it to the school and the principal put sanitary towels in the school. The women avoid wearing belts, because we are asked to take them off at checkpoints. We don't want to be asked to strip or take off part of our clothes, and there's no female soldiers in our particular checkpoint. Sometimes women buy underwear and then soldiers ask us to open our bags. It's embarrassing. Sometimes the bottom of our shoes are metal, so the metal detectors go off.

Sometimes they ask us to take off our head scarves or jackets. One girl had a short-sleeved T-shirt beneath her jacket. The soldier insisted that she take off her coat. The girl didn't want to, and the soldier said to her, 'You are hiding a knife.' A Palestinian man was there, and he said to the soldier, 'I won't leave because you might kill the girl.' I came and helped her to take off her jacket. We had to make a bad choice to prevent the worst. Afterwards, that girl started going round the back way through the olive groves to avoid the checkpoints.

Sometimes we have specific cases of women having cancers and living in the area, but Palestinian ambulances can't get to our neighbourhood. Six families left our neighbourhood because no one would ask their daughters to marry them, as people can't get access to go into our area. Even the young men in our neighbourhood get refused because people don't want their daughters to come and live in this area. Most of the youths who are from the neighbourhood go and live somewhere else. Palestinian society grows fast but in Tel Rumeida the population remains the same because young men and women get married and leave.

Do you have any final thoughts you'd like to share?

I'd like international solidarity groups to support Palestinian women who live close to the settlers, to give women opportunities for projects in their homes, because women have to stay home to protect themselves. The best form of solidarity is to support our existence on our lands, which is getting more difficult day by day. Tel Rumeida used to be a home for thousands of families, but due to the realities of settler violence and military closure we are now just 130 families, all fighting a daily struggle for survival and existence. It is a moral and political responsibility for all of us not to let Israeli settler movements win, and to maintain Palestinian existence. We have a lot of creativity and ideas that could support our shrinking community but we lack the means.

So, many families live off the olive harvest season. But even that is under threat because Israeli settlers' attacks escalate during this season. They hope to drive us out of our home through attacking our means of living and economy. Some of the olive fields we have here go back to Roman times and we ache when we see the trees being attacked as part of the Zionist reprisal techniques against us. If we have enough support we can coordinate for members of our community to protect these harvests and help maintain our existence on the land.

All women have their suffering. Every time our tears dry we get more tears. But despite all the difficulties, we continue smiling. I hope that I am succeeding in showing the voice of Palestinian society from a woman's perspective, because it is always the men who talk about this. Now my camera is my weapon.

APPENDICES

Map showing the location of each woman's home in Palestine

Haifa
Lama Suleiman

Tulkarem
Diana Khwaelid

Bil'in
Rana Abu Rahmah,
Ghada Hamdan

Jabalia refugee camp
Shahd Abusalama,
Shrouq Aila

Aida refugee camp
Shatha Abu Srour

Bethlehem
Lina Nabulsy
Sireen Khudairy

Gaza City
Ayah Al-Ghazzawi,
Samah Fadil

Al-Khalil
Faiza Abu Shamsiyah

Khan Yunis
Mona Al-Farra

Events (in chronological order)

Ottoman rule: Palestine was captured by the Ottoman Empire in 1516 and remained, save for a brief period of Egyptian rule, part of that empire until 1917.

British Mandate: the British captured Jerusalem in 1917 and assumed control over Palestine formally in 1922. The mandate was officially terminated in 1948.

Balfour Declaration: In 1917, shortly after the establishment of the British Mandate over Palestine—and after Zionist lobbying—British foreign secretary Arthur Balfour made the following statement: 'His Majesty's government view with favour the establishment in Palestine of a national home for the Jewish people, and will use their best endeavours to facilitate the achievement of this object.' This was a green light for the international Zionist movement to begin its attempts to colonise Palestine in earnest.

Zionist migration: In 1903, there were about 25,000 Jewish people in Palestine, and 500,000 Arabs. The Zionist movement encouraged Jewish migration to Palestine, and this migration was sanctioned by the British Mandate rulers of Palestine. By 1931, the Jewish population of Palestine was 175,000. By 1941, it was 474,000.[1]

Guerilla war by Zionist militias: From 1931, Zionist militias were set up, demanding a Jewish state in all of historic Palestine. These militias attacked Palestinians and also waged a guerilla war against British troops.[2]

1 Institute for Middle East Understanding (IMEU), 'Timeline: The Palestinian Nakba (Catastrophe) & Establishment of Israeli Apartheid', IMEU, May 8, 2013, https://imeu.org/article/the-nakba-65-years-of-dispossession-and-apartheid.

2 IMEU, 'Timeline'.

Palestinian revolt: Palestinians rose up against British rule and Zionist colonisation in 1936. The British army and British colonial police force defeated the revolt in 1939, with the help of Zionist militias.[3]

Nakba: The term 'al Nakba' (the catastrophe) is used by Palestinians to describe the ethnic cleansing of Palestine by Zionist militias, which led to the establishment of Israel in 1948. However, in many Western textbooks and historiographies it is described as the Israeli 'War of Independence'. The Nakba is marked every year on May 15, the day after Israel marks its 'Independence Day'.

Approximately 750,000 Palestinians became refugees in 1948; the homes they were displaced from were colonised.[4] At least 418 Palestinian villages were destroyed in the Nakba.[5]

Military rule in Israel: After Israel was established in 1948, the Palestinians who remained there lived under military rule until 1966.[6]

The 1967 War: An attack by Israel against its Arab neighbours—Egypt, Syria, and Jordan—that resulted in Israel occupying East Jerusalem, the West Bank and Gaza Strip, as well as Egypt's Sinai Peninsula and the Syrian Golan. The popular mainstream Israeli term for this event is the Six-Day War, a term which celebrates Israel's supposed military superiority.

Naksa: The Arabic name given to the 1967 war, meaning 'setback' or 'defeat'. During the Naksa 300,000 Palestinians became refugees.[7]

The 1973 War: A coordinated but unsuccessful attempt by Egypt and Syria to win back the territories that had been taken by Israel in the 1967 war. It is popularly known as the Yom Kippur War, but, as with the 1967 war, this terminology creates a false narrative portraying Israel as the benign defender against Arab aggression.

---

3 IMEU, 'Timeline'.

4 IMEU, 'Timeline'.

5 'The 418 Destroyed Villages of Palestine', *Palestine-Israel Journal* 5, no. 2 (1998), https://pij.org/articles/224/the-418-destroyed-villages-of-palestine.

6 Adel Manna, 'Palestinians Under Military Rule in Israel, 1948–1966', *Interactive Encyclopedia of the Palestinian Question*, https://www.palquest.org/en/highlight/14340/palestinians-under-military-rule-israel-1948-1966.

7 Zena Al Tahhan, 'The Naksa: How Israel Occupied the Whole of Palestine in 1967', Al Jazeera, June 4, 2018, https://www.aljazeera.com/features/2018/6/4/the-naksa-how-israel-occupied-the-whole-of-palestine-in-1967.

The hostilities paved the way for the 1978 Camp David Accords which resulted in the Sinai Peninsula being handed back to Egypt.

Black September: The name given to the 1970 Jordanian military operation which kicked the Palestine Liberation Organisation (PLO) out of Jordan.

1982 Israeli attack on Lebanon: The Israeli military invaded Lebanon, attacking the PLO's infrastructure and presence there. The attacks were indiscriminate, killing up to 20,000 people.[8] Israel's assault led to the US-brokered evacuation of PLO fighters from Beirut.

Sabra and Shatila Massacre: After the evacuation of PLO fighters, Israel's proxy Lebanese militia, the Phalange, massacred up to 3,500 Palestinians living in Sabra and Shatila refugee camps, in coordination with the Israeli military. The UN later declared the massacre, on September 16–18, 1982, as an 'act of genocide'.[9]

Israeli occupation of Lebanon: After the siege of Beirut, Israeli forces maintained an occupation of southern Lebanon. This led to a guerilla war, led by the Iran-backed Hezbollah militia. As a result, Israeli troops withdrew from Lebanon in 1999.

Intifada: The name given to the two Palestinian popular uprisings against the Israeli occupation during 1987–93, and 2000–2005. Literally translated, Intifada means 'shaking off'.

Oslo Accords: A set of agreements, signed in 1993, between the late PLO leader Yasser Arafat and the then Israeli prime minister Yitzhak Rabin. The accords, brokered by the Clinton administration in the US, were announced with much fanfare to the international community as the first step towards a Palestinian state and peace in the Middle East. In reality, they merely cemented Israel's occupation of the West Bank and Gaza Strip, and legitimised the system of apartheid that Palestinians are forced to endure daily.

The accords were supposed to be a statement of principles before planned 'final status talks', which never reached any agreement. Thus the Oslo process did nothing to address the problem of Israel's illegal settlements and effectively derailed any attempt to

8 'The 1982 Israeli Invasion of Lebanon: The Casualties', *Race & Class* 9, no. 4 (April 1983).

9 Al Jazeera Staff, 'Sabra and Shatila Massacre: What Happened in Lebanon in 1982?', Al Jazeera, September 16, 2022, https://www.aljazeera.com/news/2022/9/16/sabra-and-shatila-massacre-40-years-on-explainer.

pave the way for the return of the Palestinian refugees scattered across the Middle East.

Palestinian Authority (PA): The Palestinian Authority was established—with very limited powers—as a consequence of the Oslo Accords in 1994.

Disengagement from Gaza: In 2005, after the fierce Palestinian armed resistance of the Second Intifada, illegal Israeli colonies in Gaza were dismantled by Israel, and the settlers relocated, many of them to the West Bank. Israeli troops withdrew to the edges of the strip.[10]

Split between Fatah and Hamas: In 2006, Hamas beat Fatah in the Palestinian Legislative Council (PLC) elections in the West Bank and Gaza. Israel responded by refusing to recognise the Hamas administration, and preventing the transfer of customs duties to the PA.[11]

Fatah also refused to recognise the results of the election, and conflict between the two parties ensued. The fighting resulted in over six hundred deaths, Hamas retained control of the Gaza Strip and Fatah took control of the Palestinian Authority in the West Bank.[12]

Since then, the Hamas government in Gaza has faced international isolation and boycott, while the unelected Fatah administration in the West Bank has been backed by the US and EU.

Legislative Council elections have not been held in either the West Bank or Gaza since 2006. In the West Bank, the PA has violently suppressed members of Hamas, as well as other Palestinian political parties.[13]

In Gaza, Hamas has also arrested Fatah members. Both parties have violently crushed any popular dissent against them.[14]

---

10 Rebecca Stead, 'Remembering Israel's "Disengagement" from Gaza', *Middle East Monitor*, August 15, 2019, https://www.middleeastmonitor.com/20190815-remembering-israels-disengagement-from-gaza.

11 Stead, 'Remembering Israel's "Disengagement" from Gaza'.

12 'Over 600 Palestinians Killed in Internal Clashes Since 2006', *Ynetnews.com*, June 6, 2007, http://www.ynetnews.com/articles/0,7340,L-3409548,00.html.

13 Patrick Strickland, 'Accusations of Torture as PA Detains Hundreds of Hamas Activists', *Electronic Intifada*, July 9, 2015, https://electronicintifada.net/blogs/patrick-strickland/accusations-torture-pa-detains-hundreds-hamas-activists.

14 'Palestine: Authorities Crush Dissent', *Human Rights Watch*, October 23, 2018, https://www.hrw.org/news/2018/10/23/palestine-authorities-crush-dissent.

Attacks on Lebanon and Gaza in 2006: Israel attacked southern Lebanon in 2006, killing 1,300 people.[15] At the same time, Israel attacked Gaza killing 425 Palestinians, including 85 children.[16]

Siege of Gaza: The economic blockade and military strikes carried out by Israel on the Gaza Strip since 2007 effectively render it an open-air prison. Both Human Rights Watch and Amnesty International have denounced the siege as illegal, with most of Gaza's inhabitants living in poverty and shut off from the outside world.

Israel controls all but one of Gaza's four borders, and Egypt operates similar policies on the fourth. Limited amounts of goods are allowed to pass in and out of the strip, and 90 percent of industry had shut down even before the genocidal attacks escalated in October 2023. This has been coupled with regular Israeli air strikes targeting factories, universities, and schools, aimed at destroying the infrastructure and institutions needed to build Palestinian livelihoods.

Attempts to break the siege: There have been many international attempts to break the siege of Gaza. Convoys of vehicles have attempted to bring aid and medicine to the strip via Egypt's Rafah crossing, and several attempts have been made to break the siege by sea. Some of these have been successful. For example, in 2008, two boats carrying international activists reached Gaza.[17] In 2009 a convoy of aid from the UK successfully entered Gaza through Egypt.[18]

In 2010, Israel attacked a Turkish aid ship bound for Gaza, killing ten people.[19] Despite this, international attempts to break

15 Robert Fisk, 'Lebanon's Pain Grows by the Hour as Death Toll Hits 1,300', *The Independent*, August 17, 2006, https://www.independent.co.uk/voices/commentators/fisk/robert-fisk-lebanon-s-pain-grows-by-the-hour-as-death-toll-hits-1-300-412170.html.

16 'Indiscriminate Fire', *Human Rights Watch*, June 30, 2007, https://www.hrw.org/report/2007/06/30/indiscriminate-fire/palestinian-rocket-attacks-israel-and-israeli-artillery#_ftn59.

17 Al Jazeera and Agencies, 'Boats Reach Gaza Despite Blockade', *Palestine Chronicle*, August 23, 2008, https://www.palestinechronicle.com/boats-reach-gaza-despite-blockade; Free Gaza Movement https://www.freegaza.org.

18 'Aid Convoy Enters Gaza Strip', Al Jazeera, March 9, 2009, https://www.aljazeera.com/news/2009/3/9/aid-convoy-enters-gaza-strip.

19 Patrick Keddie, 'Remembering the Mavi Marmara Victims', Al Jazeera, July 21, 2016, https://www.aljazeera.com/news/2016/7/21/remembering-the-mavi-marmara-victims.

the siege by sea have continued but have failed to reach Gaza.[20] However, several successful land convoys to Gaza have been organised.[21]

In June 2025 the *Madleen*, part of the Freedom Flotilla, attempted to break Israel's siege once again. The vessel was targeted by Israeli drones and then intercepted in international waters with its crew arrested and deported from Israel before they could reach Gaza.

Also in June 2025, the Sumud Convoy of solidarity activists from northern African countries was blocked from continuing to Gaza by Libyan authorities, and a simultaneous separate initiative—the Global March to Gaza—was stopped by Egyptian forces, before activists from some eighty countries got close to the Egypt-Gaza Rafah crossing.

2008–9 attack on Gaza: Israel launched a massive assault on Gaza—dubbed Operation Cast Lead—killing 1,167 people, including 318 children. Schools and hospitals were bombed, and the Israeli military used banned munitions such as white phosphorus.[22]

2012 attack on Gaza: Israel launched a new invasion of Gaza—named Operation Pillar of Cloud—killing 171 people, including 34 children.[23] The majority of people were killed by unpiloted drones.[24]

2014 attack on Gaza: This intense military operation killed 2,204 Palestinians, including 526 children, in fifty days of bombing during summer 2014.[25]

Jerusalem Intifada: The Jerusalem Intifada—or the Knife Intifada—is the name of the outpouring of Palestinian resistance in 2015

20 '35 Boats Challenge Israeli Naval Blockade of Gaza in Ten Years—2008 through 2018', Freedom Flotilla Coalition, June 3, 2017, https://legalcasesagainstisraelattacksoncivilianboatstogaza.wordpress.com/2017/06/03/31-boats-challenge-israeli-naval-blockade-of-gaza.

21 'Miles of Smiles Convoy to Gaza', *Middle East Monitor*, February 20, 2014, https://www.middleeastmonitor.com/20140220-miles-of-smiles-convoy-to-gaza.

22 '4 Years Since Operation Cast Lead', Palestinian Centre for Human Rights, December 27, 2012, https://www.pchrgaza.org/en/4-years-since-operation-cast-lead.

23 Al Mezan Center for Human Rights, *Statistical Report on: Persons Killed and Property Damaged in the Gaza Strip the Israeli Occupation Forces during 'Operation Pillar of Cloud'*, November 14–21, 2012, http://www.mezan.org/en/uploads/files/17207.pdf.

24 'Elbit Systems: Company Profile', *Corporate Watch*, February 6, 2019, https://corporatewatch.org/elbit-systems-company-profile-2.

25 '50 Days: More than 500 Children: Facts and Figures on Fatalities in Gaza, Summer 2014', B'Tselem, July 20, 2016, https://www.btselem.org/press_releases/20160720_fatalities_in_gaza_conflict_2014.

and 2016 in East Jerusalem and the West Bank, which manifested itself in stabbings of Israeli soldiers and settlers, and citizens.[26]

Great March of Return: In March 2018, Palestinians began demonstrating at the wall that surrounds the Gaza Strip. Tens of thousands of people participated in the protests, which lasted for two years. The demonstrators were demanding that Palestinian refugees be allowed to return to their lands, and that Israel end its siege of Gaza. Demonstrators broke through the barrier into Israel many times.[27]

The Israeli military responded by firing at the demonstrators with live ammunition, and dropping tear gas from drones. 217 demonstrators were killed, including 48 children.[28]

2021 attack on Gaza and uprising across Israel / historic Palestine: In May 2021 Israeli troops opened fire on Palestinians demonstrating against Israeli colonists invading the Al-Aqsa Mosque compound. Jerusalem's Al-Aqsa is the third most holy site in the world for Muslims. The attack—coupled with Israel's ethnic cleansing policies in the East Jerusalem neighbourhood of Sheikh Jarrah—provoked rage across Palestine, sparking demonstrations by Palestinians all across Israel and the West Bank. The military fired on and killed demonstrators.

Israeli far-right extremist mobs carried out lynchings of Palestinians in the street inside Israel, and an Israeli settler in the West Bank city of Hebron shot a Palestinian woman dead.[29]

After the attack on Al-Aqsa, armed resistance groups in Gaza launched rockets on Tel Aviv. This was presumably just the reaction Israel was intending to provoke, and the Israeli military launched air attacks on Gaza killing 247 Palestinians, including 66 children in just eleven days.[30]

---

26 'Why the Knife Intifada?', *Middle East Monitor*, December 10, 2015, https://www.middleeastmonitor.com/20151210-why-the-knife-intifada.

27 Active Stills, 'Great March of Return: Six Months of Protests in the Gaza Strip', Al Jazeera, September 27, 2018, https://www.aljazeera.com/gallery/2018/9/27/great-march-of-return-six-months-of-protests-in-the-gaza-strip.

28 Al Mezan, 'Attacks on Unarmed Protesters at the 'Great March of Return' Demonstrations', https://www.mezan.org/en/uploads/files/15952354571567.pdf.

29 *IMEMC News*, 'Updated: Israeli Colonist Kills A Palestinian Woman In Hebron', May 19, 2021, https://imemc.org/article/israeli-colonist-kills-a-palestinian-woman-in-hebron.

30 Palestinian Centre for Human Rights, 'Cease-Fire Reached After 11 Days of IOF Aggression on Gaza', May 21, 2021, https://pchrgaza.org/cease-fire-reached-after-11-days-of-iof-aggression-on-gaza.

October 7, 2023, attack on Israel: Hamas fighters alongside other resistance groups broke through Israel's 'Iron Wall'—the fence that forcibly separates people in Gaza from the rest of the world. The Israeli death toll was 1,139, although some were killed by the response of the Israeli forces. Some 373 were Israeli soldiers, 71 were citizens of other countries, and 36 were children. Hamas fighters also took 240 men, women, and children hostage.

Hamas's attack was unprecedented, as was the group's ability to breach Israel's intelligence and security capabilities.[31] Hamas leaders reported that they had warned Israeli officials and 'anyone who would listen', that there would be an imminent attack due to Israel's tightening grip over Gaza, the West Bank, and the region, including its efforts to normalise relations with Arab countries.[32] At the time of the attack, a normalisation deal was being negotiated with Saudi Arabia.

Gaza genocide: On October 8, 2023, Israel began a fierce retaliation, bombarding the Gaza Strip. Five days later it launched a ground invasion. On October 21, Israeli forces dropped leaflets over northernmost districts of Gaza ordering people to evacuate immediately. On November 16, the UN warned that what was happening in Gaza was a 'genocide in the making'.[33]

Despite several International Court of Justice (ICJ) cases and arrest warrants for Prime Minister Benjamin Netanyahu and Defence Minister Yoav Gallant by the International Criminal Court, the genocide in Gaza continues with impunity. Israeli forces systematically and repeatedly target hospitals, schools, universities, UN buildings, shelters, mosques, churches, refugee camps, water towers, sewage and waste facilities, electricity, telephone and Wi-Fi infrastructure, residential apartment blocks, and homes. Israeli forces systematically and repeatedly target women

---

31 Al Jazeera, 'Analysis: Is Hamas a More Sophisticated Force Than Israel Imagined?', October 10, 2023, https://www.aljazeera.com/features/2023/10/10/analysis-is-hamas-a-more-sophisticated-force-than-israel-imagined.

32 Electronic Intifada, 'What Did 7 October Achieve?', February 5, 2024, https://electronicintifada.net/content/what-did-7-october-achieve/44396.

33 OHCHR, 'Gaza: UN Experts Call on International Community to Prevent Genocide Against the Palestinian People', https://www.ohchr.org/en/press-releases/2023/11/gaza-un-experts-call-international-community-prevent-genocide-against.

and children, people trying to collect aid, doctors, journalists, academics, and charity and community workers.

International institutions and human rights organisations have been slow to recognise the crimes being carried out in Gaza. Amnesty International only recognised the genocide in late 2024.

A ceasefire—flouted numerous times by Israel—came into effect on January 19, 2025. Israel officially ended the two-month-long ceasefire on March 18, 2025, killing hundreds in the first days of its renewed bombing campaign. At the time of publication, the genocide is ongoing and intensifying.

Attack on Lebanon: Cross-border fire between Israel and Lebanon's Hezbollah fighters increased in frequency when Israel began its 2023 bombardment of Gaza. On September 17 and 18, 2024, Israel drastically escalated its conflict with Hezbollah by detonating explosives concealed in pagers and walkie-talkies carried by Hezbollah members. On September 23, Israel began a bombing campaign in the country. On October 1, Israeli forces began a ground invasion of southern Lebanon. They razed many border villages to the ground, and assassinated several senior Hezbollah figures.

A sixty-day ceasefire between Israel and Hezbollah came into fragile effect on November 27, 2024, after almost 4,000 Lebanese people had been killed.

Operation Iron Wall: In February 2025, as Israel faced pressure to maintain the Gaza ceasefire, a large-scale operation began in the West Bank. As of February 26, more than 40,000 residents of the refugee camps of Jenin and Tulkarem had been displaced and prevented from returning home. Tanks were deployed in West Bank cities for the first time in more than two decades.

2025 attack on Iran: Just days before planned talks between Iran and the US on Iranian nuclear disarmament, Israel's surprise attack on June 13 began with targeted assassinations of several nuclear scientists and military leaders. Iran responded with missile and drone attacks on Israel. US President Donald Trump approved the use of US bombers to hit Iranian nuclear facilities. Israel and the US warned citizens of Iran's capital, Tehran, to evacuate. Over 800 Iranians were killed and 24 Israelis before an Iran-Israel ceasefire was announced on June 24, 2025.

Places

West Bank: The West Bank is part of historic Palestine. From the end of the 1948 war through to the 1967 war the West Bank was annexed by Jordan, and Palestinians living there became Jordanian citizens. It was the Jordanian authorities who coined the term 'West Bank'. The Israeli state often refers to the West Bank as 'Judea and Samaria', names for areas of the Kingdom of Israel referred to in the Bible. The West Bank has a population exceeding 3.2 million, including 389,250 Israeli settlers (with a further 375,000 settlers living in occupied East Jerusalem).[1]

The West Bank has been under Israeli military occupation since 1967. Mahmoud Abbas's Palestinian Authority has some very limited control over some areas of the West Bank (see the section below on Areas A, B, and C).

On January 21, 2025, Israeli forces began a large-scale military operation in the West Bank just two days after the start of the temporary ceasefire in Gaza. Some 261 people have been killed in air strikes since October 2023 in the West Bank. Killings by Israeli military and Israeli settlers have increased, there are now an average of four settler attacks a day,[2] and the Israeli military has forcibly displaced over 40,000 people from refugee camps in the north of the West Bank.

East Jerusalem: Jerusalem was divided in 1948, in the aftermath of the war of ethnic cleansing that had been waged by Zionist militias.

1 World Population Review, 'West Bank Population 2025', https://worldpopulationreview.com/regions/west-bank.

2 Al Jazeera, 'Mapping 1,800 Israeli Settler Attacks in the Occupied West Bank Since October 7th', https://www.aljazeera.com/news/2025/1/22/mapping-1800-israeli-settler-attacks-in-the-occupied-west-bank-since-october-7.

East Jerusalem came under the control of Jordan until its conquest and occupation by Israel in 1967.

In 1967, the Israeli state annexed 70,000 dunums (a dunum is equivalent to an acre) of West Bank land to East Jerusalem, and applied Israeli law there. In effect, this was an attempt at the annexation of East Jerusalem to Israel. This annexation was against international law, and the territory is internationally considered to be under military occupation. Israel prevents free movement of Palestinians from the West Bank to East Jerusalem, and its policies in East Jerusalem are intended to marginalise Palestinian communities and push Palestinians out.[3]

In 2018, US President Trump caused international uproar and protests across Palestine when he officially recognised Jerusalem as Israel's capital and opened a US embassy there.

1948 Palestine: The areas of historic Palestine—amounting to 78 percent—which were incorporated into the state of Israel when the British Mandate ended in 1948, prior to the 1949 armistice between Israel, Lebanon, Egypt, Jordan, and Syria. These lands had been seized during the ethnic cleansing of 1947–49. Prior to the ethnic cleansing campaign, Zionists controlled less than 6 percent of historic Palestine.

Israel's population now stands at 10 million. This figure includes at least 2 million Palestinian citizens of Israel.

Gaza: The Gaza Strip is a small area of land which is part of historic Palestine. It is around twenty-five miles long and six miles wide, located to the southwest of Israel, and bordering Egypt and the Mediterranean Sea. It is home to more than two million Palestinians. After the ethnic cleansing of 1948, Gaza was controlled by Egypt until 1967, when it was invaded and militarily occupied by Israel.

Today it is politically controlled by Hamas, while its borders with Israel are tightly controlled by the Israeli military. This restricts Palestinian freedom of movement and the flow of goods entering, thus suffocating the Gazan economy and causing immense suffering to its people.

---

3 B'Tselem, 'East Jerusalem', November 11, 2017, updated January 27, 2019, https://www.btselem.org/jerusalem.

Although Israeli settlers and troops were withdrawn from the centre of Gaza in 2005, Israel's continued domination of the strip through its military infrastructure on Gazan soil, and constant drone surveillance and aerial attacks, amount to a continuation of the occupation.

Gaza is now unrecognizable due to the Israel-led genocide which began in October 2023. The infrastructure is rubble and will take decades to rebuild. Israeli politicians have repeatedly and overtly spoken of their plans to ethnically cleanse Palestinians and to build new settlements in Gaza.

Occupied Syrian Golan: An area in the southwest of Syria which was occupied by Israel during the 1967 war, driving more than 100,000 Syrians from their homes. It is commonly referred to as the 'Golan Heights', a term which ignores Israel's colonial land grab. In 1967, nearly 140,000 Syrians lived in the Golan. Today around 29,000 Israeli settlers live there.[4] In 1981 the Golan Heights Law extended Israeli law to the occupied Syrian Golan, a de facto annexation which is not accepted by the majority of Syrian residents of the Golan or by international law.[5]

In December 2024, Israel seized a new 'buffer zone' in the region after the Bashar al-Assad regime in Syria was toppled. At the time of writing, conflict is ongoing as Israel attempts to occupy more land in Syria.

Occupied Palestinian Territories: The Palestinian areas under Israeli military occupation: the West Bank, East Jerusalem, and Gaza.

Occupied Territories: All areas under Israeli military occupation (the Occupied Palestinian Territories and the Occupied Syrian Golan).

Areas A, B, and C: Under the Oslo agreement of 1993, the West Bank was divided into three zones of control. 'Area A' was supposed to be under Palestinian control, 'Area B' jointly controlled, and 'Area C' under Israeli jurisdiction. The agreement was supposed to be an interim measure until the creation of a Palestinian state which would take control of all three areas, save for any areas

4 Al-Marsad, 'Illegal Settlements', February 24, 2022, https://golan-marsad.org/illegal-settlements.

5 BBC, 'Golan Heights Profile', August 29, 2023, https://www.bbc.co.uk/news/world-middle-east-14724842.

which were subject to future agreements between the parties. Of course, the agreement never progressed to the next stage, but more than thirty years later the Israeli regime is still twisting the interim measures to its advantage. State policy is to stamp out Palestinian livelihoods and communities in Area C, and give the land to the expanding Israeli settlements. Palestinians are barred, to all intents and purposes, from building any new structures, and this is enforced by the home demolition policy.[6]

Al-Khalil: The Palestinian name for Hebron. Al-Khalil means 'friend' or 'the friend of God', referring to Abraham who is thought to be buried there. Similarly, the Israeli term Hebron (or Hevron as it is also known) derives from the Hebrew word for friend.

Since 1968, Israeli settlers have established a number of colonies in the city centre of Hebron, and have launched a campaign of violence against Palestinian residents. The city was separated into two zones of control—H1 and H2—in the 1997 Hebron Agreement (which followed the massacre of 29 Palestinians by a Zionist at the Ibrahimi Mosque).[7] The Israeli military retained control of security matters in H2, which includes a large part of the city centre. In H2, 34,000 Palestinians now experience extreme limits on their freedom of movement and intense violence and harassment from the thousands of Israeli soldiers occupying the city.[8]

Jordan Valley: Located in the eastern part of the West Bank, with the southern parts bordering the Dead Sea and the eastern parts bordering the Jordan River. The valley comprises 28.5 percent of the entire West Bank and has the most fertile land in the region. It was occupied by the Israeli army in 1967 and is now home to thirty Israeli colonies, an increasing number of settlement outposts, and twenty-four military bases of varying sizes. The Palestinian population of the Jordan Valley stood at 320,000 in the period between 1948 and 1967, and has fallen to just 65,000 today. Despite the

---

6 Eliza Egret and Tom Anderson, with Amy Hall, *Resisting the Demolitions: A BDS Handbook*, (Shoal Collective, 2019), 19, https://corporateoccupation.org/wp-content/uploads/sites/34/2019/03/resisting-demolitions-ebook-v2.pdf..

7 Mapping the Apartheid, 'Area H1, H2, ' accessed June 6, 2025, https://www.hebronapartheid.org/index.php?glossary=area-H1-H2.

8 B'Tselem, 'Hebron City Center', November 11, 2017, updated May 26, 2019, https://www.btselem.org/hebron.

large number of settlements, the settler population is only around 11,000. Ninety-five percent of the valley is controlled by Israel for the benefit of industrial settler agriculture.[9]

Israeli politicians have announced their intention to annex the Jordan Valley to Israel.[10] This plan received support from the Trump administration in the US in 2020,[11] and may well do so again.

Al-Quds: The Arabic name for Jerusalem, meaning 'The Holy'.

Naqab: The Palestinian name for the desert situated in what is now southern Israel (known as the Negev in Hebrew), covering around 60 percent of the country's land mass.

Kibbutz/Moshav: Israeli-Jewish collective communities traditionally based on agriculture. The kibbutz movement was one of the largest recipients of stolen Palestinian land after 1948.[12]

The Green Line: The line demarcating the furthest advance of Zionist troops into Palestinian territory in 1949.

We use 'within' or 'inside' the 'Green Line' in this book to describe land taken by Israel in 1948, and 'beyond' the 'Green Line', to describe land taken from within the West Bank, Gaza, and the Occupied Syrian Golan since then.

The apartheid wall: The Israeli apartheid state began building the apartheid wall inside the West Bank in 2002. It is not built along the Green Line, but instead cuts deep into the West Bank. The wall cuts off Palestinians from their land, and is intended as a massive land grab. In 2004, the International Court of Justice ruled the construction of the wall illegal.[13]

Gaza wall and partition corridors: The original barrier around Gaza was built in 1971, but was largely torn down by Palestinians at the beginning of the Second Intifada. In 2001, a one-kilometre

9 Asharq Al Awsat, 'PLO Official: Israel Controls 95% of Jordan Valley', March 25, 2020, https://english.aawsat.com/home/article/2198431/plo-official-israel-controls-95-jordan-valley.

10 MEE staff, 'Israel's Planned Annexation of the Jordan Valley: Why It Matters', *Middle East Eye*, May 22, 2020, https://www.middleeasteye.net/news/palestine-israel-annexation-jordan-valley-why-it-matters.

11 Al Jazeera, 'Israel's Annexation Plan for Occupied West Bank', June 28, 2020, https://www.aljazeera.com/news/2020/6/28/explainer-israels-annexation-plan-for-occupied-west-bank.

12 Ilan Pappé, *The Ethnic Cleansing of Palestine,* (Oneworld, 2006).

13 Stop the Wall: Palestinian Grassroots Anti-Apartheid Wall Campaign, 'The Wall', https://stopthewall.org/the-wall.

'buffer zone' was added between Israel and Gaza, along with new observation posts.[14]

In 2021, Israel finished constructing its 'iron wall' along the route of the existing wall, spanning 40 miles.[15] The iron and steel wall took 3.5 years to complete and includes machine gun towers, a naval barrier, command and control rooms, a radar system, and a sensor-equipped underground barrier. Next to the wall is a 'buffer zone' patrolled by armoured vehicles. The wall was breached by Hamas fighters on October 7, 2023, and crossed by hundreds of civilians, some of whom were shot and killed by Israeli forces.

In October 2024, Israeli forces began demolishing hundreds of buildings east to west of the strip to construct a new military dividing line in northern Gaza, which looked set to further isolate those who still lived there.[16] However, in February 2025, some 100,000 people who had been forced from the north in October 2023 began returning home.

Israeli forces also constructed the Netzarim Corridor in February 2024, a road splitting north from south Gaza, and the Philadelphi Corridor in August 2024, which runs the length of Gaza's border with Egypt.[17]

Gaza marine barrier: In 2018, the Israeli Ministry of Defence began constructing a thirty-seven-mile-long marine barrier off the coast of the Gaza Strip.[18]

Palestinian refugee camps: Set up by the United Nations Relief and Works Agency (UNWRA) in the West Bank, Jordan, Lebanon, Syria, and the Gaza Strip to accommodate the Palestinian refugees

---

14 'Background: The Separation Barrier', Al Jazeera, July 6, 2008, https://www.aljazeera.com/news/2008/7/6/background-the-separation-barrier.

15 Andrei Popoviciu and Lubna Masarwa, 'Gaza: What the Iron Wall Built by Israel Means for Besieged Palestinians', *Middle East Eye*, December 11, 2021, https://www.middleeasteye.net/news/israel-iron-wall-gaza-palestinians-siege.

16 Benedict Garman, Nick Eardley, and Matt Murphy, 'Israel Building New Military Dividing Line Across Gaza, Satellite Images Suggest', *BBC Verify*, November 28, 2024, https://www.bbc.co.uk/news/articles/cp8x324vromo.

17 Abdirahim Saeed, Tom Spencer, Paul Brown, and Richard Irvine-Brown, 'IDF Completes Road Across Width of Gaza, Satellite Images Show', *BBC Arabic* and *BBC Verify*, March 10, 2024, https://www.bbc.co.uk/news/world-middle-east-68514821; Benedict Garman, 'Satellite Images Show How Israel Is Paving Key Gaza Road', *BBC Verify*, September 7, 2024, https://www.bbc.co.uk/news/articles/cewlqpk9e99o.

18 Middle East Monitor, 'Israel Builds Marine Barrier North of Gaza', May 29, 2018, https://www.middleeastmonitor.com/20180529-israel-builds-marine-barrier-north-of-gaza.

of 1948 and 1967.[19] These camps still exist today, although they are more like permanent, overcrowded, and under-resourced, urban neighbourhoods than camps.

19 UNRWA, 'Palestine Refugees', https://www.unrwa.org/palestine-refugees.

Glossary

Palestinian-Israeli: Palestinian citizens of Israel. The term 'Arab-Israeli' is commonly used in the mainstream and Zionist media. But the term is often considered offensive, as the term 'Arab' is used in Zionist colonial discourse to negate the existence of Palestinians, and imply that Palestinian Arabs are not indigenous to the land.

Bedouin: Primarily nomadic or semi-nomadic pastoralists who live in the deserts of North Africa and the Middle East. Prior to the state of Israel, the majority of Palestinian Bedouin resided in the south of Palestine, in Bir Saba, the Naqab, and south of Al-Khalil. Whilst most of the Palestinian Bedouin were forcefully expelled from these areas by Zionist forces during the Nakba, around 130,000 remain in the Naqab.

Many of those expelled from the south now live in the West Bank, including in Area C communities in the Jordan Valley.

Zionism: An ideology and political movement—whose origins date from the nineteenth century—which asserts that all Jewish people constitute one nation, and advocates the creation of a Jewish homeland. The movement is a white supremacist, racist, and settler colonialist one, aimed at creating a state which acts only for its Jewish citizens, and attempts to erase diversity. David Ben Gurion—a Zionist leader in British mandate Palestine who became Israel's first prime minister—encapsulated Zionism's aim when he said: 'We must expel Arabs and take their place.'[1]

1 Adam Horowitz, '"We Must Expel Arabs and Take Their Place": Institute for Palestine Studies Publishes 1937 Ben-Gurion Letter Advocating the Expulsion of Palestinians', *Mondoweiss*, March 28, 2012, https://mondoweiss.net/2012/03/we-must-expel-arabs-and-take-their-place-institute-for-palestine-studies-publishes-1937-ben-gurion-letter-advocating-the-expulsion-of-palestinians.

Palestinian refugees: The Palestinians who have been forced to leave their homes since 1948, and their descendants. There are now more than 8.36 million Palestinian refugees worldwide.[2]

Right of Return: One foundation of the Palestinian struggle is that the refugees and their descendants have the right to return home. This right is also guaranteed to Palestinian refugees in international law.[3]

Palestinian refugees have been prevented from returning to Palestine since 1948. The injustice of this is highlighted by the fact that all peoples of Jewish heritage worldwide have a right to citizenship in Israel.

Home demolition: Israel's demolitions are concentrated in key strategic areas of planned settlement expansion. Hundreds of Palestinian communities in these areas are under threat of being wiped off the map by these demolitions. Between October 7, 2023, and October 15, 2024, Israel demolished 1,787 Palestinian buildings including 800 inhabited homes, in the West Bank alone.[4] Satellite images collected in Gaza on December 1, 2024, showed that 69 percent of structures had been destroyed or damaged during the genocide.[5]

Palestinian communities face home demolitions within the Green Line too. For example, the Palestinian Bedouin village of Al-Araqib had been demolished 235 times as of January 2025.[6]

In Gaza, the Israeli military carries out demolitions of agricultural land and property in the area alongside Israel's wall, which runs along three sides of the Gaza Strip. The Israeli military has declared this area a 'buffer zone', and does not allow building there.

---

2 IMEU, 'Quick Facts: Palestinian Refugees', June 19, 2024, https://imeu.org/article/quick-facts-palestinian-refugees.

3 War on Want, 'The Palestinian Right of Return', June 13, 2018, https://waronwant.org/news-analysis/palestinian-right-return.

4 Palestinian Information Centre, '1,787 Israeli Demolitions in the West Bank Since the Start of the War on Gaza', October 17, 2024, https://english.palinfo.com/reports/2024/10/17/327165.

5 UNITAR, 'UNOSAT Gaza Strip Comprehensive Damage Assessment', December 13, 2024, https://unosat.org/products/4047.

6 Palestinian Information Centre, 'Israel Razes Araqib Village in Negev for 235th Time', January 29, 2025, https://english.palinfo.com/news/2025/01/29/333085.

Targeted assassinations: Israel neither confirms nor denies its targeted assassination policy, but its assassinations are estimated to have killed nearly 3,000 Palestinians since 1948.[7]

Drones: Israel deploys small remote-controlled drones, some of which are called quadcopters, both for 24/7 surveillance of Gazans and to maim and kill. Small drones increased in number and have become louder after the start of the Gaza genocide. Some play sounds of crying babies and distressed women to draw Palestinians out of their shelters.[8] Israel also deploys larger unpiloted military aircraft. Thousands of people in Gaza have been killed in Israeli drone strikes, often in targeted assassinations.[9]

Apartheid: A term meaning a legal system of racial segregation, originally used to describe the policies of the White National Party governments ruling South Africa between 1948 and 1994. The term is often used by Palestinians to describe the system of racial discrimination established by the Israeli apartheid regime.

The definition of the crime of apartheid, as defined by the 2002 Rome Statute of the International Criminal Court, is inhumane acts 'committed in the context of an institutionalised regime of systematic oppression and domination by one racial group over any other racial group or groups and committed with the intention of maintaining that regime'.[10]

Ethnic cleansing: A term which was first used to refer to the atrocities committed during the breakup of the former Yugoslavia. It has been defined as a 'policy of a particular group of persons to systematically eliminate another group from a given territory on the basis of religious, ethnic or national origin. Such a policy involves violence and is very often connected to military operations. It is to be achieved by all possible means, from discrimination to extermination.'[11]

---

7 Charlie Hoyle, 'A History of Violence', *New Arab*, November 28, 2018, https://www.newarab.com/analysis/history-violence-israels-targeted-assassinations.

8 Shahd Safi, 'Drones Above Gaza', We Are Not Numbers, November 13, 2023, https://wearenotnumbers.org/drones-above-gaza.

9 Euro-Med Human Rights Monitor, 'Gaza: Israeli Army Expands Its Use of Quadcopters to Kill More Palestinian Civilians', June 4, 2024, https://euromedmonitor.org/en/article/6357/Gaza:-Israeli-army-expands-its-use-of-quadcopters-to-kill-more-Palestinian-civilians.

10 ICRC, 'Article 7— Crimes Against Humanity', https://ihl-databases.icrc.org/en/ihl-treaties/icc-statute-1998/article-7.

11 Drazen Petrovic, 'Ethnic Cleansing—An Attempt at Methodology', *European Journal of International Law* 5, no. 3 (1994): 342–59.

In *The Ethnic Cleansing of Palestine*, written in 2006, Israeli historian Ilan Pappé argues that this term can be used to describe the destruction of villages, expulsions, murder, and massacres which occurred during the colonisation of Palestine during 1947–49.

The term 'ethnic cleansing' has been criticised by some anti-racists because the word 'cleansing' could imply the presence of impurity. However, 'ethnic cleansing' has become a popular term used by many Palestinians to describe a particular type of colonialism and the actions of armed Zionist groups before, during, and after the 1948 war. The term can also be applied to the expulsions of Palestinians from the West Bank during the 1967 war. Acts of ethnic cleansing are perpetrated on a routine basis by the Israeli apartheid regime. The Gaza genocide has seen the largest and most overt attempt to ethnically cleanse Palestinians from northern Gaza, and indeed all of Gaza, since the 1948 Nakba, with many calling it the second Nakba.

Judaization: the systematic attempts by the Israeli government and settler organisations to move Jewish people into areas populated by Palestinians in order to alter the demographic balance in favour of Jewish people. Judaization is often coupled by the systematic denial of services to Palestinian areas in Israel and East Jerusalem.

Normalisation: A term used to describe the promotion of economic, cultural, and political ties with Israel with the aim of consolidating Israeli occupation and apartheid. US foreign policy is designed to promote normalisation of relations between Arab states and Israel. In August 2020, US pressure brokered a normalisation deal between Israel, the United Arab Emirates, and Bahrain, called the Abraham Accords.[12]

Settlement/colony: This refers to the transfer and settlement of an Israeli-Jewish population into the occupied territories of the West Bank, East Jerusalem, and Syrian Golan. It covers not only the act of settling in these territories, but is also used to describe the communities which Israeli-Jewish settlers establish.

The Rome Statute of the International Criminal Court defines the 'transfer, directly or indirectly, by the Occupying Power of

12 Yara Hawari, 'The Betrayal', *New Internationalist*, March 6, 2024, https://newint.org/politics/2024/betrayal-israel-arab-normalisation.

parts of its own civilian population into the territory it occupies' as a war crime.[13] More than 764,250 Israeli-Jewish settlers currently live in the West Bank and East Jerusalem, whilst an estimated 31,000 live in the occupied Syrian Golan.[14] These settlements are not only built on land stolen from Palestinians and Syrians, but they also continually rob nearby local populations of other resources such as water.

However, the Israeli state and Israeli Zionist organisations also pursue a process of land grabs and colonisation within Palestinian areas inside the Green Line. This occurs, for example, in the Naqab where Israeli state policy and parastatal organisations like the Jewish National Fund are being used to evict Palestinian Bedouins and replace their communities with Jewish-only kibbutzim. In reality there is little difference between Israeli policies of colonisation within the Green Line and Israel's settlement policy in the West Bank.

Popular Committees: Palestinian committees which began to be set up in the First Intifada, aimed at creating a grass-roots platform for mass popular resistance to the Israeli occupation, carrying out popular education, and building Palestinian autonomy. The concept of popular committees has been key to the popular struggle since the Second Intifada too, but the Palestinian Authority has tried hard to control and dominate them.[15]

Popular resistance/struggle: A term used by Palestinians for the non-military struggle against the occupation. This includes weekly demonstrations in many towns and villages against Israel's apartheid wall and settlements, the Boycott, Divestment and Sanctions movement, hunger strikes by Palestinian prisoners in Israeli jails, and other forms of direct action.

---

13 ICC, 'Rome Statute of the International Criminal Court', https://www.icc-cpi.int/publications/core-legal-texts/rome-statute-international-criminal-court.

14 Al-Marsad, 'Illegal Settlements', February 24, 2022, https://golan-marsad.org/illegal-settlements; Al Jazeera, 'Israel Approves Plan to Surge Settler Population in Occupied Golan Heights', December 15, 2024, https://www.aljazeera.com/news/2024/12/15/israel-approves-plan-to-surge-settler-population-in-occupied-golan-heights'; B'Tselem, 'Settlements', November 11, 2017, updated January 16, 2019, https://www.btselem.org/settlements.

15 Tayseer Arouri, 'From the Streets to the Committees, Palestine Is United', *New Arab*, December 12, 2014, https://www.newarab.com/analysis/streets-committees-palestine-united.

WCNSF—Wounded Child, No Surviving Family: An acronym coined at the start of the Gaza genocide, an aggression where children make up over 40 percent of the casualties.[16]

16 OCHA, 'Gaza: Children Under Attack', January 17, 2024, https://www.unocha.org/news/gaza-children-under-attack.

Palestinian Movements

Fatah: (meaning 'to conquer' or 'opening') was set up in the late 1950s by Yasser Arafat and Khalil al-Wazir, also known as Abu Jihad. FATH is the inverted acronym of the Harakat al-Tahrir al-Watani al-Filastini or 'Palestine National Liberation Movement'.

Fatah obtained support from the Syrian state in the 1960s, and based itself out of Damascus. It carried out its first military operation against Israel in 1964 and established itself formally in 1965.

Fatah's initial strategy was a military one, but it has officially pursued a two-state solution since the late 1980s, and was the primary Palestinian political party involved in the 1993 Oslo Accords.

Yasser Arafat, Fatah's co-founder, became the first president of the Palestinian Authority in 1994,[1] following its creation in 1993, after the Palestine Liberation Organisation and Israel signed the Oslo Accords.

The PA's authority is extremely limited; its role is essentially to manage the Palestinian population on behalf of the Israeli occupiers.

Mahmoud Abbas became the PA president in 2005, after Arafat's death. Abbas has publicly stated that he does not support the right to return for Palestinian refugees (although he later tried

1 Rifat Odeh Kassis, 'Fatah Chapter Closed: Creating a Palestinian National Congress', *Electronic Intifada*, March 27, 2006, https://electronicintifada.net/content/fatah-chapter-closed-creating-palestinian-national-congress/5913.

to backtrack).[2] On his watch, the PA has collaborated with Israeli security forces and arrested and tortured Palestinians.[3]

Hamas won the Palestinian Legislative Council elections in 2006, but Fatah refused to cede control to them in the West Bank. Fatah, with Abbas remaining as the PA president, has held unelected power over the PA in the West Bank ever since.

Palestine Liberation Organisation (PLO): The PLO was formed in 1964, and had its roots in the Arab nationalist movements that were prominent at the time. The PLO's stated goal was the liberation of all of historic Palestine through armed struggle.[4] It is an umbrella organisation, which is recognised by many Arab states as the sole representative of the Palestinian people. The PLO was granted observer status by the UN General Assembly in 1974.[5]

Structurally, the PLO is made up of an Executive Committee, the Central Committee and the Palestinian National Council (PNC), which was envisaged as the Palestinian parliament in exile.

Initially based in Jordan, the PLO was forced to move to Lebanon after conflict with the Jordanian state in the 'Black September' of 1970. In 1982, the organisation was forced to move again to Tunisia, after Israel's invasion of Lebanon. The PLO's fighters had to remain in military camps in different Arab countries until the conclusion of the Oslo Accords.[6]

Throughout its history, the PLO has been dominated by Fatah. In 1988 the PLO issued the Palestinian Declaration of Independence, which signified its support for a two-state solution,

---

2 Ali Abunimah, 'There's Nothing New in Mahmoud Abbas' and the PLO's Renunciation of Palestinian Refugee Rights', *Electronic Intifada*, November 4, 2012, https://electronicintifada.net/blogs/ali-abunimah/theres-nothing-new-mahmoud-abbas-and-plos-renunciation-palestinian-refugee-rights.

3 Ali Abunimah, 'Will Mahmoud Abbas Really Stop PA Collaboration with Israel?', *Electronic Intifada*, May 20, 2020, https://electronicintifada.net/blogs/ali-abunimah/will-mahmoud-abbas-really-stop-pa-collaboration-israel; Jamal Juma', 'PA Repression Feeds Flames of Palestinian Discontent', *Electronic Intifada*, July 3, 2012, https://electronicintifada.net/content/pa-repression-feeds-flames-palestinian-discontent/11456.

4 'The PLO Charter', IRIS, July 1968, https://iris.org.il/plochart.htm.

5 Agence France Presse, 'United Nations Observer Status: Facts', *The National*, November 27, 2012, https://www.thenationalnews.com/world/mena/united-nations-observer-status-facts-1.438482.

6 Kassis, 'Fatah Chapter Closed'.

and called for a Palestinian state to be established beyond the Green Line.[7]

Popular Front for the Liberation of Palestine: Founded by George Habash following the Israeli colonial occupation of 1967, the PFLP is a Marxist-Leninist communist resistance movement, set up with the aim of guerilla warfare to achieve the liberation of Palestine. According to the PFLP's *Strategy for the Liberation of Palestine*: 'The aim of the Palestinian liberation movement is to establish a democratic national state in Palestine in which both Arabs and Jews will live as citizens with equal rights and obligations and which will constitute an integral part of the progressive democratic Arab national presence living peacefully with all forces of progress in the world.'[8]

By the 1970s the PFLP had firmly pledged allegiance to the Soviet Union.[9]

The front has played an important part in the Palestinian armed struggle, orchestrating several plane hijackings in the 1970s. The group maintained connections with international guerilla resistance movements such as Germany's Red Army Faction and the Kurdistan Workers' Party (PKK).[10]

The PFLP initially joined the PLO, but left in 1993 in opposition to the PLO's support of a two-state solution. The front opposed the Oslo Accords and boycotted the Palestinian National Council. However, since 2000, the front has made statements

---

7 'Palestinian Declaration of Independence', *Interactive Encyclopedia of the Palestine Question*, November 15, 1988, https://www.palquest.org/en/historictext/9673/palestinian-declaration-independence.

8 Popular Front for the Liberation of Palestine, *The Strategy for the Liberation of Palestine* (Foreign Languages Press, 2017), https://foreignlanguages.press/wp-content/uploads/2020/08/S08-PFLP-Strategy-Lib-Palestine-7th-Printing.pdf.

9 As'ad AbuKhalil, 'George Habash's Contribution to the Palestinian Struggle', *Electronic Intifada*, January 30, 2008, https://electronicintifada.net/content/george-habashs-contribution-palestinian-struggle/7332.

10 'A Brief History of the RAF', *Arm the Spirit—For Revolutionary Resistance*, August 31, 2017, https://armthespiritforrevolutionaryresistance.wordpress.com/2017/08/31/a-brief-history-of-the-raf; Kurdistan Solidarity Network, 'A Time for Us to Follow on Their Footsteps ... Palestine, Kurdistan and the Martyrs of May', *Autonomy News*, May 19, 2021, https://autonomynews.org/a-time-for-us-to-follow-on-their-footsteps-palestine-kurdistan-and-the-martyrs-of-may.

accepting the 'reality' of the need to accept a solution based on the Green Line.[11]

Democratic Front for the Liberation of Palestine: In 1969, Nayef Hawatmeh and Yasser Abed Rabbo broke from the PFLP to form the openly Maoist Democratic Front for the Liberation of Palestine (DFLP). The DFLP joined the PLO, and has helped to form the PLO's 'two-state solution' stance. The front has been involved in armed resistance to the Israeli occupation from various bases in Jordan, the Golan Heights, and Lebanon.[12] The DFLP provided training to the PKK, as well as Nicaragua's Sandinistas.[13]

The front declined in influence—as did the PFLP—after the collapse of the Soviet Union, but stood candidates in the Palestinian presidential elections in 2005 and in the most recent elections for the PLC (way back in 2006).[14]

Islamic Jihad: Palestinian Islamist movement formed in the early 1980s, inspired by the 1978–79 Islamic revolution in Iran. *Jihad* means to struggle. Islamic Jihad's aim was to build a bridge between the Palestinian nationalist movement and Islam. The movement has played a substantial role in armed resistance against the Israeli occupation.[15] The organisation is not part of the PLO and rejects the Oslo Accords. Islamic Jihad was backed by Syria's Assad regime as well as the Iranian state and is allied with Hamas.[16]

---

11 'Profile: Popular Front for the Liberation of Palestine (PFLP)', *BBC News*, November 18, 2014, https://www.bbc.co.uk/news/world-middle-east-30099510.

12 Maher Charif, 'The Democratic Front for the Liberation of Palestine—DFLP', *Interactive Encyclopedia of the Palestine Question*, https://palquest.palestine-studies.org/en/highlight/23611/democratic-front-liberation-palestine-%E2%80%93-dflp.

13 Aliza Marcus, *Blood and Belief: The PKK and the Kurdish Fight for Independence* (NYU Press, 2007).

14 Arjan El Fassed, 'Election Day Polls Open in Gaza', *Electronic Intifada*, January 9, 2005, https://electronicintifada.net/content/election-day-polls-open-gaza/5409.

15 Mohammad Ataie, 'How the Axis of Resistance Is Shaping the Middle East', *Middle East Eye*, October 14, 2024, https://www.middleeasteye.net/big-story/middle-east-axis-resistance-shaping-how.

16 Ahmad Abu Amer, 'Islamic Jihad Seeks to Renew Ties with Damascus', *Al-Monitor*, January 14, 2019, https://www.al-monitor.com/originals/2019/01/palestine-islamic-jihad-meet-syria-regime-support.html; Al Jazeera, 'How have Palestinian groups reacted to the ouster of Syria's al-Assad?', December 9, 2024, https://www.aljazeera.com/news/2024/12/9/how-have-palestinian-groups-reacted-to-the-ouster-of-syrias-al-assad.

Hamas: An acronym of Harakat al-Muqawamah al-ʾIslamiyyah, or the 'Islamic Resistance Movement', Hamas has its roots in Egypt's Islamist Muslim Brotherhood. The organisation was founded as a separate entity in 1987, after the outbreak of the first Palestinian Intifada.[17]

Hamas won the Palestinian Legislative Council elections in 2006, but Fatah would not cede control to them. Hamas retained control of the Gaza Strip, which it has governed ever since.

An economic boycott of Gaza has been in place by European powers, Israel, and the US since 2007—as punishment for electing Hamas—but financial and material support has come from state and non-state supporters globally including Iran, Turkey, and donors in the Gulf States.[18]

Internationally, the movement was initially based in Jordan until 1999 when they were kicked out. Hamas then operated out of Syria—supported by Bashar Al-Assad—until 2012, when Al-Assad accused Hamas operatives of supporting the armed resistance against his regime.[19] Hamas currently has an international presence in Qatar and Turkey and close relations with Hezbollah in Lebanon.[20] The organisation rejects all agreements with Israel, including the Oslo Accords.[21]

BDS Movement: The Boycott, Divestment and Sanctions (BDS) movement is a Palestinian civil society movement, which came together after the international BDS call was made by hundreds

---

17 Khaled Hroub, *Hamas: A Beginner's Guide* (Pluto Press, 2010).

18 Kristen Chick, 'Briefing: The Motives and Aims of Hamas', *Christian Science Monitor*, May 13, 2009, https://www.csmonitor.com/World/Middle-East/2009/0513/p06s19-wome.html; Zvi Bar'el, 'Turkey May Provide Hamas with $300 Million in Annual Aid', *Haaretz*, January 28, 2012, https://www.haaretz.com/2012-01-28/ty-article/turkey-may-provide-hamas-with-300-million-in-annual-aid/0000017f-f487-d044-adff-f7ff19be0000.

19 Ahmad Abu Amer, 'Islamic Jihad Seeks to Renew Ties with Damascus', *Al-Monitor*, January 14, 2019, https://www.al-monitor.com/originals/2019/01/palestine-islamic-jihad-meet-syria-regime-support.html.

20 David Gritten and Rushdi Abualouf, 'Hamas Leaders No Longer in Doha but Office Not Permanently Closed, Qatar Says', BBC, November 19, 2024, https://www.bbc.co.uk/news/articles/c86qd99nqgyo; Ragip Soylu, 'Turkey: Hamas Has Not Moved Offices to Country, Sources Say', *Middle East Eye*, November 18, 2024, https://www.middleeasteye.net/news/hamas-hasnt-moved-its-offices-turkey-turkish-officials-say; Al Jazeera Staff, 'What Is Hezbollah?', Al Jazeera, October 10, 2023, https://www.aljazeera.com/news/2023/10/10/what-is-hezbollah-a-look-at-the-lebanese-armed-group-backing-hamas.

21 MEE Staff, 'Hamas in 2017: The Document in Full', *Middle East Eye*, May 2, 2017, https://www.middleeasteye.net/news/hamas-2017-document-full.

of Palestinian grass-roots groups—as well as groups representing the occupied Syrian population in the Golan. The call was made in 2005, in the aftermath of the ruling from the International Court of Justice that Israel's apartheid wall was illegal. It reads:

> We, representatives of Palestinian civil society, call upon international civil society organizations and people of conscience all over the world to impose broad boycotts and implement divestment initiatives against Israel similar to those applied to South Africa in the apartheid era. We appeal to you to pressure your respective states to impose embargoes and sanctions against Israel. We also invite conscientious Israelis to support this Call, for the sake of justice and genuine peace.
>
> These non-violent punitive measures should be maintained until Israel meets its obligation to recognise the Palestinian people's inalienable right to self-determination and fully complies with the precepts of international law by:
>
> 1. Ending its occupation and colonization of all Arab lands and dismantling the Wall
> 2. Recognizing the fundamental rights of the Arab-Palestinian citizens of Israel to full equality; and
> 3. Respecting, protecting and promoting the rights of Palestinian refugees to return to their homes and properties as stipulated in UN resolution 194.[22]

The Boycott National Committee was set up to represent the interests of the groups who had signed the call.

Since 2005, the BDS movement has grown into a global force to be reckoned with. Israel's Ministry of Strategic Affairs has mounted international efforts to counter the effects of BDS internationally, and to encourage states to criminalise BDS activity.[23]

---

22 BDS, 'Palestinian Civil Society Call for BDS', July 9, 2005, https://bdsmovement.net/call.

23 Nathan Thrall, 'BDS: How a Controversial Non-Violent Movement Has Transformed the Israeli-Palestinian Debate', *The Guardian*, August 14, 2018, https://www.theguardian.com/news/2018/aug/14/bds-boycott-divestment-sanctions-movement-transformed-israeli-palestinian-debate.

About the Contributors

Shoal Collective is an independent co-operative of writers and researchers. We produce news articles, investigations, and analysis as a contribution to, and a resource for, movements that are attempting to bring about social and political change.

Huwaida Arraf is a Palestinian American activist and lawyer who co-founded the International Solidarity Movement (ISM), a Palestinian-led organisation committed to resisting the long-entrenched and systematic oppression and dispossession of the Palestinian population, using non-violent direct-action methods and principles.

ABOUT PM PRESS

PM Press is an independent, radical publisher of critically necessary books for our tumultuous times. Our aim is to deliver bold political ideas and vital stories to all walks of life and arm the dreamers to demand the impossible. Founded in 2007 by a small group of people with decades of publishing, media, and organizing experience, we have sold millions of copies of our books, most often one at a time, face to face. We're old enough to know what we're doing and young enough to know what's at stake. Join us to create a better world.

PM Press
PO Box 23912
Oakland, CA 94623
www.pmpress.org

PM Press in Europe
europe@pmpress.org
www.pmpress.org.uk

FRIENDS OF PM PRESS

These are indisputably momentous times—the financial system is melting down globally and the Empire is stumbling. Now more than ever there is a vital need for radical ideas.

In the many years since its founding—and on a mere shoestring—PM Press has risen to the formidable challenge of publishing and distributing knowledge and entertainment for the struggles ahead. With hundreds of releases to date, we have published an impressive and stimulating array of literature, art, music, politics, and culture. Using every available medium, we've succeeded in connecting those hungry for ideas and information to those putting them into practice.

Friends of PM allows you to directly help impact, amplify, and revitalize the discourse and actions of radical writers, filmmakers, and artists. It provides us with a stable foundation from which we can build upon our early successes and provides a much-needed subsidy for the materials that can't necessarily pay their own way. You can help make that happen—and receive every new title automatically delivered to your door once a month—by joining as a Friend of PM Press. And, we'll throw in a free T-shirt when you sign up.

Here are your options:

- **$30 a month** Get all books and pamphlets plus a 50% discount on all webstore purchases

- **$40 a month** Get all PM Press releases (including CDs and DVDs) plus a 50% discount on all webstore purchases

- **$100 a month** Superstar—Everything plus PM merchandise, free downloads, and a 50% discount on all webstore purchases

For those who can't afford $30 or more a month, we have **Sustainer Rates** at $15, $10, and $5. Sustainers get a free PM Press T-shirt and a 50% discount on all purchases from our website.

Your Visa or Mastercard will be billed once a month, until you tell us to stop. Or until our efforts succeed in bringing the revolution around. Or the financial meltdown of Capital makes plastic redundant. Whichever comes first.

Revolution at Point Zero Housework, Reproduction, and Feminist Struggle, Second Edition

Silvia Federici

ISBN: 978-1-62963-797-6
$17.95 256 pages

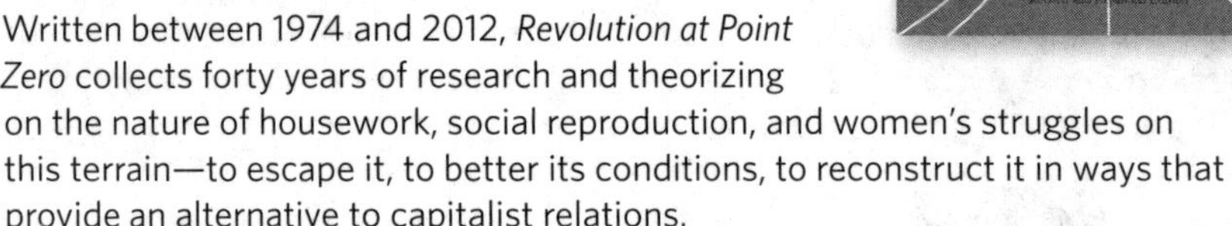

Written between 1974 and 2012, *Revolution at Point Zero* collects forty years of research and theorizing on the nature of housework, social reproduction, and women's struggles on this terrain—to escape it, to better its conditions, to reconstruct it in ways that provide an alternative to capitalist relations.

Indeed, as Federici reveals, behind the capitalist organization of work and the contradictions inherent in "alienated labor" is an explosive ground zero for revolutionary practice upon which are decided the daily realities of our collective reproduction.

Beginning with Federici's organizational work in the Wages for Housework movement, the essays collected here unravel the power and politics of wide but related issues including the international restructuring of reproductive work and its effects on the sexual division of labor, the globalization of care work and sex work, the crisis of elder care, the development of affective labor, and the politics of the commons.

This new and expanded edition contains two previously unpublished essays by the author.

"Federici has become a crucial figure for young Marxists, political theorists, and a new generation of feminists."
—Rachel Kushner author of *The Flamethrowers*

"Federici's attempt to draw together the work of feminists and activist from different parts of the world and place them in historical context is brave, thought-provoking and timely. Federici's writing is lucid and her fury palpable."
—*Red Pepper*

"Real transformations occur when the social relations that make up every.day life change, when there is a revolution within and across the stratifica.tions of the social body. . . . Silvia Federici offers the kind of revolutionary perspective that is capable of revealing the obstacles that stand in the way of such change."
—Feminist Review

Nourishing Resistance: Stories of Food, Protest, and Mutual Aid

Edited by Wren Awry with a Foreword by Cindy Barukh Milstein

ISBN: 978-1-62963-992-5
$20.00 192 pages

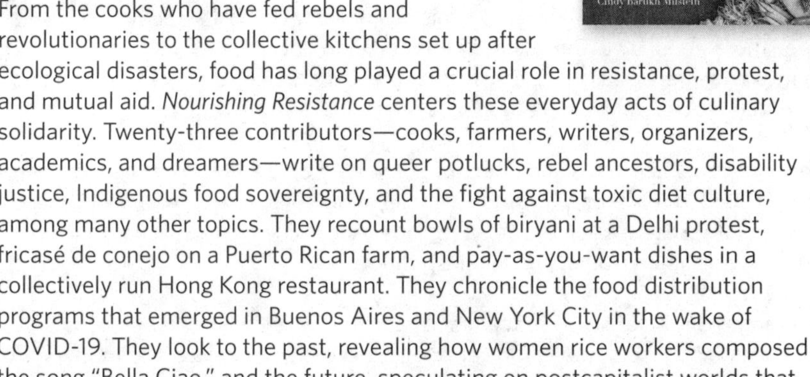

From the cooks who have fed rebels and revolutionaries to the collective kitchens set up after ecological disasters, food has long played a crucial role in resistance, protest, and mutual aid. *Nourishing Resistance* centers these everyday acts of culinary solidarity. Twenty-three contributors—cooks, farmers, writers, organizers, academics, and dreamers—write on queer potlucks, rebel ancestors, disability justice, Indigenous food sovereignty, and the fight against toxic diet culture, among many other topics. They recount bowls of biryani at a Delhi protest, fricasé de conejo on a Puerto Rican farm, and pay-as-you-want dishes in a collectively run Hong Kong restaurant. They chronicle the food distribution programs that emerged in Buenos Aires and New York City in the wake of COVID-19. They look to the past, revealing how women rice workers composed the song "Bella Ciao," and the future, speculating on postcapitalist worlds that include both high-tech collective farms and herbs gathered beside highways.

Through essays, articles, poems, and stories, *Nourishing Resistance* argues that food is a central, intrinsic part of global struggles for autonomy and collective liberation.

"This collection of essays offers invaluable frameworks and inspirational models on how to get food out of capitalist markets and into the hands and stomachs of all. They fiercely demonstrate how the harvesting, growing, preparing, cooking, sharing, and eating of food has shaped and reshaped our cultures, created the social conditions for conviviality, and helped to break the seclusion and alienation that racist capitalist patriarchies organize. A must read for all who dream of keeping practices of commoning alive."
—Silvia Federici, author of *Re-enchanting the World: Feminism and the Politics of the Commons*

"A thoughtfully assembled, refreshingly global collection of radical voices who urge us to reimagine the meaning of the phrase 'food is political.'"
—Mayukh Sen, author of *Taste Makers: Seven Immigrant Women Who Revolutionized Food in America*

All of Me: Stories of Love, Anger, and the Female Body

Edited by Dani Burlison

ISBN: 978-1-62963-705-1
$19.95 240 pages

With women's anger, empowerment, and the critical importance of intersectional feminism taking center stage in much of the dialogue happening in feminist spaces right now, an anthology like this has never been more important. The voices in this collection of essays and interviews offer perspectives and experiences that help women find common ground, unity, and allyship.

Through personal essays and interviews about what it is like to live as a woman (cis + trans) in this modern world—with all of our love, anger, complexities, and desires for justice—*All of Me: Stories of Love, Anger, and the Female Body* includes vulnerable, painful truths and bold inspiration.

This anthology is for seasoned feminists and young feminists alike—anyone looking to find inspiration in radical activism, creativity, healing, and more. This book covers topics of social and economic justice, creativity, racism, transgender perspectives, sexuality, sex work, addiction and recovery, reproductive rights, assault, relationship dynamics, families, fitting and not fitting in, radical self-care, witchcraft, and more.

If love and anger are two sides of the same coin, for women there are worlds to be explored with every flip of that coin. Readers will find a glimpse into those worlds in the pages of *All of Me*.

Contributors include Silvia Federici, Michelle Cruz Gonzales, Ariel Gore, Laurie Penny, Lidia Yuknavitch, Christine No, Kandis Williams, Vatan Doost, Deya, Phoenix LeFae, Anna Silastre, Michel Wing, Bethany Ridenour, Lorelle Saxena, Airial Clark, Patty Stonefish, Nayomi Munaweera, Melissa Madera, Margaret Elysia Garcia, Leilani Clark, Ariel Erskine, Wendy-O Matik, Kara Vernor, Starhawk, adrienne maree brown, Gerri Ravyn Stanfield, Sanam Mahloudji, Melissa Chadburn, Avery Erickson, and Milla Prince.

The Art of Freedom: A Brief History of the Kurdish Liberation Struggle

Havin Guneser with an Introduction by Andrej Grubačić and Interview by Sasha Lilley

ISBN: 978-1-62963-781-5 (paperback)
978-1-62963-907-9 (hardcover)
$16.95/$39.95 192 pages

The Revolution in Rojava captured the imagination of the left, sparking a worldwide interest in the Kurdish Freedom Movement. *The Art of Freedom* demonstrates that this explosive movement is firmly rooted in several decades of organized struggle.

In 2018, one of the most important spokespersons for the struggle of Kurdish Freedom, Havin Guneser, held three groundbreaking seminars on the historical background and guiding ideology of the movement. Much to the chagrin of career academics, the theoretical foundation of the Kurdish Freedom Movement is far too fluid and dynamic to be neatly stuffed into an ivory-tower filing cabinet. A vital introduction to the Kurdish struggle, *The Art of Freedom* is the first English-language book to deliver a distillation of the ideas and sensibilities that gave rise to the most important political event of the twenty-first century.

The book is broken into three sections: "Critique and Self-Critique: The rise of the Kurdish freedom movement from the rubbles of two world wars" provides an accessible explanation of the origins and theoretical foundation of the movement. "The Rebellion of the Oldest Colony: Jineology—the Science of Women" describes the undercurrents and nuance of the Kurdish women's movement and how they have managed to create the most vibrant and successful feminist movement in the Middle East. "Democratic Confederalism and Democratic Nation: Defense of Society Against Societycide" deals with the attacks on the fabric of society and new concepts beyond national liberation to counter it. Centering on notions of "a shared homeland" and "a nation made up of nations," these rousing ideas find deep international resonation.

Havin Guneser has provided an expansive definition of freedom and democracy and a road map to help usher in a new era of struggle against capitalism, imperialism, and the State.

Their Blood Got Mixed: Revolutionary Rojava and the War on ISIS

Janet Biehl

ISBN: 978-1-62963-944-4
$27.95   256 pages

In the summer of 2012 the Kurdish people of northern Syria set out to create a multiethnic society in the Middle East. Persecuted for much of the 20th century, they dared to try to overcome social fragmentation by affirming social solidarity among all the region's ethnic and religious peoples. As Syria plunged into civil war, the Kurds and their Arab and Assyrian allies established a self-governing polity that was not only multiethnic but democratic. And women were not only permitted but encouraged to participate in all social roles alongside men, including political and military roles.

To implement these goals, Rojava wanted to live in peace with its neighbors. Instead, it soon faced invasion by ISIS, a force that was in every way its opposite. ISIS attacked its neighbors in Iraq and Syria, imposing theocratic, tyrannical, femicidal rule on them. Those who might have resisted fled in terror. But when ISIS attacked the mostly Kurdish city of Kobane and overran much of it, the YPG and YPJ, or people's militias, declined to flee. Instead they resisted, and several countries, seeing their valiant resistance, formed an international coalition to assist them militarily. While the YPG and YPJ fought on the ground, the coalition coordinated airstrikes with them. They liberated village after village and in March 2019 captured ISIS's last territory in Syria.

Around that time, two UK-based filmmakers invited the author to spend a month in Rojava making a film. She accepted, and arrived to explore the society and interview people. During that month, she explored how the revolution had progressed and especially the effects of the war on the society. She found that the war had reinforced social solidarity and welded together the multiethnic, gender-liberated society. As one man in Kobane told her, "Our blood got mixed."

"You haven't been to Rojava yet? Let Janet Biehl's graphic novel help you take your first step to the land of revolutionary hope, to North-East Syria, by providing a fascinating glimpse and thrilling insight into the most significant revolution of the 21st century. History is usually written by powerful elites and rulers, but Janet Biehl invites us to a new viewpoint. Their Blood Got Mixed *is a creative contribution to a historiography from the perspective of those who actually made it."*
—Havin Guneser, one of the spokespersons of the International Initiative "Freedom for Abdullah Öcalan—Peace in Kurdistan" and author of *The Art of Freedom*